General Assembly
Official Records
Seventy-first Session
Supplement No. 5D

A/71/5/Add.4

United Nations Relief and Works Agency for Palestine Refugees in the Near East

Financial report and audited financial statements

for the year ended 31 December 2015

and

Report of the Board of Auditors

United Nations • New York, 2016

Please recycle

Print ISSN: 1020-2439
Online ISSN: 2521-618X

Contents

Letter of transmittal

Letter dated 30 June 2016 from the Chair of the Board of Auditors addressed to the President of the General Assembly

I have the honour to transmit to you the report of the Board of Auditors on the financial statements of the United Nations Relief and Works Agency for Palestine Refugees in the Near East for the year ended 31 December 2015.

(*Signed*) Mussa Juma **Assad**
Controller and Auditor-General of the United Republic of Tanzania
Chair of the United Nations Board of Auditors

Chapter I

Report of the Board of Auditors on the financial statements: audit opinion

We have audited the accompanying financial statements of the United Nations Relief and Works Agency for Palestine Refugees in the Near East (UNRWA) for the year ended 31 December 2015, which comprise the statement of financial position (statement I), the statement of financial performance (statement II), the statement of changes in net assets/equity (statement III), the statement of cash flow (statement IV), the statement of comparison of budget and actual amounts (statement V) and the notes to the financial statements.

Responsibility of management for the financial statements

The Commissioner-General of UNRWA is responsible for the preparation and fair presentation of the financial statements in accordance with the International Public Sector Accounting Standards (IPSAS) and for such internal controls as management deems necessary to enable the preparation of financial statements that are free from material misstatement, whether due to fraud or error.

Responsibility of the auditors

Our responsibility is to express an opinion on these financial statements based on our audit. We conducted our audit in accordance with the International Standards on Auditing, which require that we comply with ethical requirements and plan and perform the audit to obtain reasonable assurance that the financial statements are free from material misstatement.

An audit involves performing procedures to obtain audit evidence about the amounts and disclosures in the financial statements. The procedures selected depend on the auditor's judgment, including an assessment of the risks of material misstatement of the financial statements, whether due to fraud or error. In making those risk assessments, the auditor considers such internal controls as are relevant to the entity's preparation and fair presentation of the financial statements in order to design audit procedures that are appropriate in the circumstances, but not for the purpose of expressing an opinion on the effectiveness of the entity's internal controls. An audit also includes evaluating the appropriateness of the accounting policies used and the reasonableness of accounting estimates made by management, as well as evaluating the overall presentation of the financial statements.

We believe that the audit evidence that we have obtained is sufficient and appropriate to provide a basis for our audit opinion.

Opinion

In our opinion, the financial statements present fairly, in all material respects, the financial position of UNRWA as at 31 December 2015 and its financial performance and cash flow for the year then ended, in accordance with IPSAS.

Report on other legal and regulatory requirements

Further to our opinion, the transactions of UNRWA that have come to our notice or that we have tested as part of our audit have, in all significant respects, been in accordance with the Financial Regulations of UNRWA and legislative authority.

In accordance with article VII of the United Nations Regulations and Rules and regulation 12.2 of the UNRWA Financial Regulations, we have also issued a long-form report on our audit of UNRWA.

(*Signed*) Mussa Juma **Assad**
Controller and Auditor-General of the United Republic of Tanzania
Chair of the United Nations Board of Auditors
(Lead Auditor)

(*Signed*) Sir Amyas C. E. **Morse**
Comptroller and Auditor-General of the
United Kingdom of Great Britain and Northern Ireland

(*Signed*) Shashi Kant **Sharma**
Comptroller and Auditor-General of India

30 June 2016

Chapter II
Long-form report of the Board of Auditors

Summary

The United Nations Relief and Works Agency for Palestine Refugees in the Near East (UNRWA) provides assistance and protection to more than 5 million registered Palestinian refugees to help them achieve their full potential in terms of human development. UNRWA employs approximately 30,890 area staff at its five fields of operations in Gaza, Jordan, Lebanon, the Syrian Arab Republic and the West Bank, as well as at its headquarters in Amman and Gaza.

UNRWA is primarily funded through voluntary contributions. During 2015, total contributions were $1,178.73 million, of which voluntary contributions were $1,130.09 million (96 per cent), and total expenses amounted to $1,333.77 million.

The Board of Auditors audited the financial statements and reviewed the operations of UNRWA for the year ended 31 December 2015 in accordance with General Assembly resolution 74 (I) and in conformity with the International Standards on Auditing. The audit was carried out through the examination of financial transactions and operations at UNRWA headquarters in Amman and at its field offices in Jordan, Gaza, Lebanon and the West Bank.

Scope of the report

The present report covers matters that, in the opinion of the Board, should be brought to the attention of the General Assembly; it has been discussed with UNRWA management, whose views have been appropriately reflected.

The audit was conducted primarily to enable the Board to form an opinion as to whether the financial statements present fairly the financial position of UNRWA as at 31 December 2015 and its financial performance and cash flows for the year then ended, in accordance with the International Public Sector Accounting Standards (IPSAS). The audit included a general review of financial systems and internal controls and a test examination of the accounting records and other supporting evidence to the extent that the Board considered necessary to form an opinion on the financial statements.

The Board also reviewed UNRWA operations under financial regulation 7.5 of the Financial Regulations and Rules of the United Nations, which allows the Board to make observations on the efficiency of the financial procedures, the accounting system, the internal financial controls and, in general, the administration and management of operations. The Board examined four key UNRWA programmes: the health programme; the education programme; the relief and social services programme; and the infrastructure and camp improvement programme. The report also includes a brief commentary on the status of implementation of the recommendations made in previous years.

Audit opinion

In the opinion of the Board, the financial statements present fairly, in all material respects, the financial position of UNRWA as at 31 December 2015 and its financial performance and cash flows for the year then ended, in accordance with IPSAS.

The Board also issued a separate unqualified audit opinion on the financial statements of the UNRWA Area Staff Provident Fund for the year ended 31 December 2015, which were prepared in accordance with the International Financial Reporting Standards. In addition, the Board performed an annual audit of the Microfinance Department and issued an unqualified opinion on its financial statements for the year ended 31 December 2015.

Overall conclusion

The Board found no material misstatements in the UNRWA financial statements. Nevertheless, as in its previous report, the Board continues to note persistent problems with the unreliability and unpredictability of revenue sources available to the Agency to deliver its core mandate to Palestine refugees in its five fields of operation. Other areas requiring immediate management intervention for improvement related to: the new enterprise resource planning system (known as REACH), results-based management, inventory, procurement and contract management, fleet management, human resource management, health programme management and information and communication technology. Those areas highlighted the need for effective internal control and monitoring of activities in the field offices and headquarters to ensure greater adherence to the regulations and technical instructions governing the Agency's operations. The Board considers that the deficiencies need to be addressed urgently in order to ensure the efficient and effective delivery of the UNRWA mandate.

Key findings

The Board has identified a number of issues that need to be considered by management in order to enhance the effectiveness of UNRWA operations. In particular, the Board highlights the key findings set out below.

Financial overview

Overall financial performance of UNRWA

The Agency's original budget was revised from $982.18 million to $1.08 billion, while the actual expenditure was $899 million resulting in unspent balance of $183.65 million, attributable mainly to the project funds. However, fluctuation and unpredictability of core resources supporting the core operations remained a problem to the Agency. For example, during the period of June to September 2015 UNRWA recorded a deficit of $101 million in its core budget, which threatened the ability to provide its services. While the donors and observers[1] of the Agency intervened to address the situation, UNRWA faces the prospect of financial difficulties in future, since its budget and cash projections for 2016 still project a budget deficit of $81.30 million.

The overall financial position of UNRWA continued to be sound as at 31 December 2015 as the current assets are 2.63 times greater than current liabilities, and the ratio of total assets to total liabilities is 1.24. However, the Agency has

---

[1] State of Palestine, the European Union and the League of Arab States.

insufficient cash reserves to meet its current liabilities under the programme budget (see table II.2). For the period under review, total revenue was $1,212.73 million (2014: $1,342.19 million) and total expenses amounted to $1,333.77 million (2014: $1,298.49 million), representing a deficit for the year of $121.05 million. The overall deficit reflects a deficit of $127.64[2] million in the programme budget, which finances the core activities of the Agency. All other funds also closed with deficits except the Microfinance Department and project fund, which closed with surpluses of $0.35 million and $9.22 million, respectively.

The deficit for the programme budget has increased substantially, from $30.38 million in 2014 to $127.64 million, an increase of 320 per cent. The reported deficit in the programme budget is mainly attributable to an amount of $158.16 million, comprising projected severance expenses of $106.48 million for the period and non-cash expenses from depreciation of $29.96 million, a loss on disposal of assets of $3.26 million, provision and write off of $18.36 million and impairment loss of $0.10 million. The projected severance expenses[3] have increased from $35.11 million in 2014 to $106.48 million owing to an increase in the rate of retirement benefit computation from 11 per cent to 12 per cent of the completed years of service and a decrease in the discount rate from 4.75 per cent to 4.32 per cent to align with the decline in the interest rate for government bonds in the market.

Results-based management

Lack of midyear results review report for 2015

UNRWA introduced the midyear results review in 2013 to complement the established annual review process in order to align results-based management best practices by proactively reviewing organizational performance in key areas and linking results with utilized resources. However, UNRWA did not produce the midyear results review report for 2015. The Board considers that the lack of midyear results review report limits the assessment of achievements and use of the financial resources, outputs, encountered challenges and the planned interventions for the subsequent six months. UNRWA attributed the failure to produce the midyear results review report for 2015 to its involvement in the preparation of operational documents including the medium-term strategy for 2016-2021 and headquarters implementation plans.

Travel management

Lack of advance ticket travel policy on air tickets booking arrangement

UNRWA did not have an advance ticket travel policy and as a result most of the tickets were booked one to five days before the dates of travel. For example, the Board found that bookings for 222 (58 per cent) out of 383 sampled air tickets were made one to five days before the dates of travel, when ticket prices are likely to be higher than those for bookings made in advance. While UNRWA attributed this deficiency to the long internal process for approving travels, the Board considers that the key problem is the lack of documented advance ticket booking policy to guide and streamline travel management approving processes.

---

[2] Note 33 (segment reporting by funds).

[3] Current period expense of the projected end of service liability under the defined benefit plan.

Information and communications technology

Lack of information and communications technology strategy

The Board noted that UNRWA does not have an information and communications technology strategy. The strategy is crucial for identifying the vision, mission and objectives as concerns information and communications technology, as well as the targeted enterprise architecture and road map to achieve them. UNRWA stated that for the past three years, the focus was on the implementation of the enterprise resource planning system and therefore an information and communications technology strategy was not developed, but it was in the process of developing a new organizational directive No. 26 (October 2015) on information and communications technology to facilitate the drafting of the strategy. The Board considers that the lack of an information and communications technology strategy exposes the Agency to risks of allocating inadequate budget and resources required to support the related infrastructure as well as delays in building information and communications technology capabilities required to support its strategic intentions and to respond in a timely manner to organizational transformation.

Information and communications technology security governance

UNRWA information security activities are distributed under various information and communications technology personnel, rather than being centralized to information and communications technology security personnel, in order for close attention to be given through an information security programme. Additionally, UNRWA has neither updated its information security policy nor developed an information security programme or assigned accountability for information security. The Board considers that the deficiencies are mainly due to the lack of a framework to guide the development and maintenance of a comprehensive information security programme and an updated information security policy, and that these may compromise the Agency's ability to protect itself from information security risks.

Monitoring of privileged access

The access control to the system requires the use of privileged access ("super user") on the domain and applications are granted to appropriate personnel, logged and reviewed by management. Nevertheless, the Board found that the following controls were lacking in relation to the accounts of privileged users for the Microfinance Department: (a) formal reviews over the audit logs and event viewer to detect any discrepancies in accessing active directory, application and database through privileged accounts; (b) independent information and communications technology security personnel to monitor privileged users' activities; and (c) procedures to guide the review of activities performed at all access levels (domain, network, system software and applications). Also, the passwords for the administrator accounts were not properly secured to support the succession plan. These deficiencies increase the risk of losing data integrity through unauthorized activities.

Main recommendations

The Board has made several recommendations based on its audit that are contained in the body of the report. The main recommendations are that UNRWA:

(a)   Design an action plan that will enable the midyear results review report to be issued on the due date and discussed in the results review participants meeting to support management decision-making;

(b)   (i) Develop a travel policy that will define the air ticketing booking arrangement; and (ii) look at ways of streamlining further the approval processes with regard to travel management so that they are completed within reasonable time;

(c)   Consider developing an information and communications technology strategy together with an enterprise architecture and road map to support UNRWA business objectives;

(d)   (i) Develop a comprehensive information security programme; (ii) update the information security policy; (iii) develop a steering committee for information security and assign accountability to ensure information security strategies are aligned with and support business objectives;

(e)   (i) Maintain an audit trail (logs) and monitor the actions of sensitive accounts and implement a "sign off" process on a periodic basis by an information security officer or a person with similar responsibilities who is independent from the information and communications technology team; (ii) define and formally document administrator accounts at all levels and ensure passwords for these administrator accounts are properly secured and kept with the Agency's management, with access to be granted in a formal process.

<table>
<tr><td colspan="2">Key facts</td></tr>
<tr><td>More than 5 million</td><td>Population of Palestinians refugees served by UNRWA</td></tr>
<tr><td>30,890</td><td>UNRWA area staff (local staff)</td></tr>
<tr><td>218</td><td>UNRWA international staff</td></tr>
<tr><td>$323.96 million</td><td>Procurement cost in 2015</td></tr>
<tr><td>500,698 students</td><td>$510.72 million spent in education programme in 2015</td></tr>
<tr><td>692</td><td>Primary and secondary education schools</td></tr>
<tr><td>9.19 million</td><td>Patients visiting UNRWA health centres annually</td></tr>
<tr><td>143</td><td>Health centres</td></tr>
<tr><td>$1.11 million</td><td>Expenditure on information and communications technology equipment for 2015</td></tr>
</table>

A. Mandate, scope and methodology

1. The United Nations Relief and Works Agency for Palestine Refugees in the Middle East (UNRWA) was established by General Assembly resolution 302 (IV) of 8 December 1949 and became operational on 1 May 1950. It is a subsidiary organ of the Assembly within the United Nations system. The mandate of UNRWA is to help Palestinian refugees achieve their full potential in terms of human development under difficult circumstances, consistent with internationally agreed goals and standards. UNRWA is one of the largest United Nations programmes, serving more than 5 million Palestinian refugees in the Gaza Strip, Jordan, Lebanon, the Syrian Arab Republic and the West Bank. UNRWA is also one of the largest employers in the Middle East, with approximately 30,890 staff, most of whom are Palestinian refugees. UNRWA has 692 schools, accommodating approximately 500,698 students and 17,862 educational staff, as well as 143 health centres across the region serving more than 9.19 million patients annually. UNRWA also assists some 280,000 of the poorest and most vulnerable refugees with special needs, including people with disabilities.

2. The Board of Auditors has audited the financial statements of UNRWA and has reviewed its operations for the year ended 31 December 2015 in accordance with General Assembly resolution 74 (I). The audit was conducted in conformity with regulation 12.2 of the Financial Regulations of UNRWA and the International Standards on Auditing. The latter standards require that the Board comply with ethical requirements and plan and perform the audit to obtain reasonable assurance as to whether the financial statements are free from material misstatement.

3. The audit was conducted primarily to enable the Board to form an opinion as to whether the financial statements present fairly the financial position of UNRWA as at 31 December 2015 and its financial performance and cash flows for the year then ended, in accordance with the International Public Sector Accounting Standards (IPSAS). This included an assessment as to whether the expenses recorded in the financial statements had been incurred for the purposes approved by

the governing body and whether revenue and expenses had been properly classified and recorded in accordance with the Financial Regulations of the Agency. The audit included a general review of financial systems and internal controls and a test examination of the accounting records and other supporting evidence to the extent that the Board considered it necessary in order to form an opinion on the financial statements.

4. In addition to the audit of the financial statements, the Board carried out reviews of UNRWA operations in accordance with regulation 7.5 of the Financial Regulations and Rules of the United Nations. Specific areas covered during audit include treasury and cash management, education programme management, health programme management, budget management, procurement and contract management, property management, relief and social services programme management, human resources management, assets management, project and programme management, results-based management and information and communications technology.

B. Findings and recommendations

1. Follow-up to previous recommendations of the Board

5. The Board noted that of the 71 outstanding recommendations as at 31 December 2014, 25 (36 per cent) had been fully implemented, 37 (52 per cent) were under implementation, 7 (10 per cent) had been reiterated, 1 (1 per cent) had been overtaken by events, while 1 (1 per cent) had not been implemented. Overall, the status of implementation indicates that the management needs to exert more efforts to implement the majority of recommendations, which are under implementation. The Board considers that this represents an improvement compared with the previous implementation rate. In 2013, 3 per cent of recommendations were fully implemented; 84 per cent were under implementation; 8 per cent were overtaken by events and 2 per cent were not implemented, and 3 per cent were reiterated. Details regarding action taken in relation to the recommendations outstanding as of 2014 are summarized in annex I.

2. Financial overview

6. In 2015, UNRWA reported total revenue of $1,212.73 million (2014: $1,342.19 million) and total expenses of $1,333.77 million (2014: $1,298.49 million), resulting in a deficit of $121.04 million.

7. The programme budget, which finances core activities, recorded revenue of $639.05 million (2014: $637.18 million) and expenses of $766.69 million (2014: $667.56 million), resulting in a deficit of $127.64 million (2014: $30.38 million). The reported deficit in the programme budget includes $158.16 million, comprising the projected severance expenses of $106.48 million for the period and non-cash expenses from depreciation of $29.96 million, loss on disposal of assets $3.26 million, provision for doubtful debts of $18.36 million and impairment loss of $0.10 million. Financial performance, by fund, is summarized in table II.1.

Table II.1
Financial performance by fund

(Millions of United States dollars)

| | Unearmarked activities | Earmarked activities | | | | | |
Description	Programme budget	Restricted funds	Microfinance Department	Emergency appeals	Projects	Inter-fund balances	Total
Revenue	639.05	16.10	9.57	418.31	180.3	(50.6)	1 212.73
Expenses	766.69	18.48	9.22	418.83	171.08	(50.53)	1 333.77
Surplus/(deficit)	**(127.64)**	**(2.38)**	**0.35**	**(0.52)**	**9.22**	**(0.07)**	**(121.04)**

Source: UNRWA financial statements for 2015.

8.   The 2015 deficits of \$2.38 million and \$0.52 million in restricted funds and emergency appeals are due to timing differences in the recognition of revenue and expenses whereby revenue was recognized in a prior year while the projects were executed and expenses accounted for in 2015.

Revenue analysis

9.   Voluntary contributions form a major part of the Agency's revenues. During 2015, UNRWA received total contributions of \$1,178.73 million (2014: \$1,321.19 million), of which \$1,132.78 million (96 per cent) represents voluntary contributions from various donors as compared to \$1,276.84 million in 2014. The remaining \$45.95 million (2014: \$44.34 million), equivalent to 4 per cent was received from the United Nations regular budget and other United Nations agencies. In comparison with the previous year, voluntary contributions decreased by \$146.75 million (11 per cent). The decrease in revenue was attributed to fewer contributions received towards the emergency appeals in 2015 compared to 2014. Appreciation of the United States dollar against other currencies in 2015 is also the cause of the decrease in the amount of United States dollar equivalency received during the year under review. A breakdown of revenues is provided in the figure below.

Voluntary contributions by source of revenue

(Thousands of United States dollars)

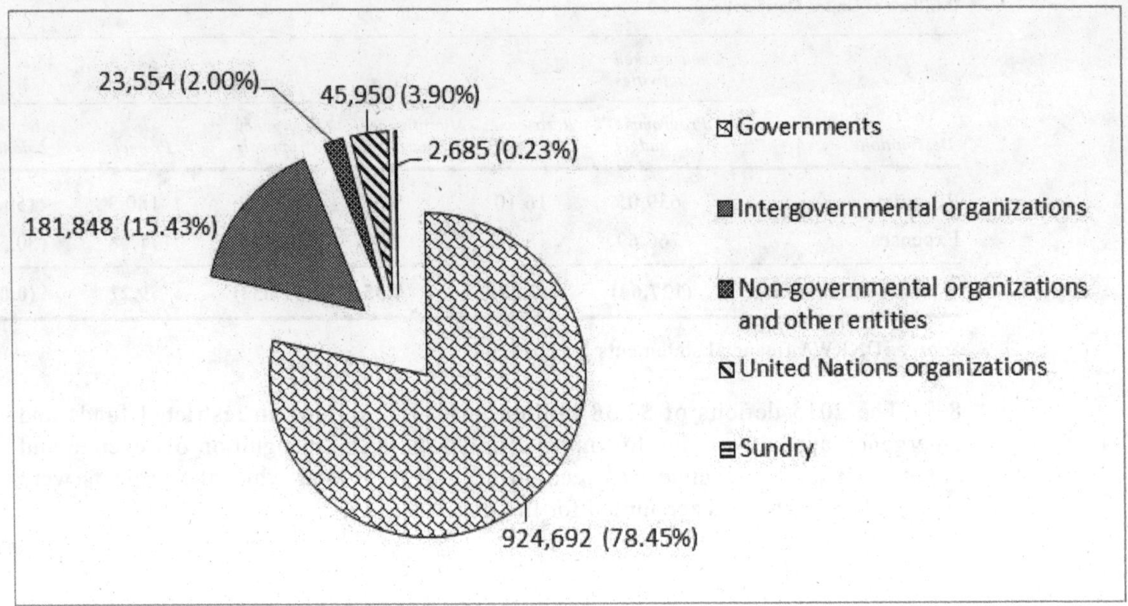

Source: Extracted from UNRWA financial statements (notes 20 and 21).

Expense analysis

10.   Total expenses increased by $35.28 million, from $1,298.49 million in 2014 to $1,333.77 million in 2015, an increase of 3 per cent. The increase in expenses is mostly attributable to the emergency appeals fund received at the end of 2014 and spent during 2015.

11.   Wages, salaries and employee benefits amounted to $709.94 million (2014: $651.50 million) or 54 per cent of the total expenses of $1,333.77 million, which is a significant portion of UNRWA expenses. The reported amount of wages, salaries and employee benefits includes area staff costs of $599.68 million (2014: $546.65 million) or 84.47 per cent and international staff of $45.15 million (2014: $43.74 million) or 6.36 per cent. The remaining balance represents UNRWA contributions to the area staff provident fund of $55.53 million (2014: $52.40 million) or 7.82 per cent, and health-related expenses of $9.58 million (2014: $8.71 million) or 1.35 per cent.

Statement of financial position

Net assets and reserves

12.   The Agency's overall net assets/equity decreased by 40 per cent from the restated balance of $328.68 million as at 31 December 2014 to $196.13 million as at 31 December 2015. The net assets/equity comprised fund balances of $191.4 million and reserves of $4.73 million. The Agency's reserve declined by 70.9 per cent from $16.26 million in 2014 to $4.73 million in 2015. The Board is concerned that the significant decline in net assets and reserves increases the risk of inability to deliver services to refugees if donors' funds are delayed.

Cash and cash equivalents

13.   The statement of financial position as at 31 December 2015 reported a cash balance of $308.78 million (2014: $305.45 million), an increase of $3.33 million (1.09 per cent). However, out of the $308.78 million, only $41.76 million (13.52 per cent) was available to the programme budget, which finances the Agency's core operations, thus creating a strain on the Agency's resources for such operations. The majority of the cash balance related to project funds ($87.83 million, 28.44 per cent) and emergency appeals ($168.67 million, 54.62 per cent), while the cash balances relating to restricted funds and the Microfinance Department were $1.55 million (0.51 per cent) and $8.98 million (2.91 per cent), respectively. UNRWA attributed the large balances of emergency appeals and project funds to the late receipt of donors' contributions for 2015 activities, which will be accounted for in 2016.

Accounts receivable

14.   The accounts receivable net of provision decreased by $8.38 million from $42.61 million in 2014 to $33.77 million in 2015. Of the $33.77 million in accounts receivable, $22.12 million (65 per cent) represents value added tax (VAT) receivables. The large portion of VAT receivables of $22.12 million (90.38 per cent) originates from the Palestinian Authority, which has been accrued for a period of 20 years, while the remaining balances of $1.66 million (7.52 per cent) and $0.46 million (2.10 per cent) come from the Governments of Israel and Lebanon, respectively. Dialogue between UNRWA and the Palestinian Authority on the recoverability of VAT receivables is still ongoing.

Inventories

15.   In response to the Board's recommendation on the need to reclassify non-inventory items as inventory in accordance with IPSAS 12, UNRWA reclassified non-inventory to inventory items as part of the transition to the new enterprise resource planning system (known as REACH). Changes made sought to enhance the visibility of all items bought by quantity and value, thereby strengthening accountability, tracking consumption for strategic sourcing analysis and integrating applications to manage inventory accurately across multiple warehouses and locations. The reclassification resulted in an increase in the opening balance of inventory by $10.80 million, from $85.56 million to $96.36 million.

Accounts payable and accruals

16.   Payables and accruals decreased by 22.25 per cent, from $86.55 million reported in 2014 to $67.29 million in 2015. The decrease in payables and accruals was mainly owing to the timely disbursement of contributions due to the Provident Fund and the timely payment of accrued salaries and other expenses.

Ratio analysis

17.   Table II.2 contains key financial ratios analysed from the financial statements, mainly from the statements of financial position and financial performance.

Table II.2
Ratios of key financial indicators

Ratio	2014 (all funds)	Programme budget 2015	2015 (all funds)
Cash/total assets[a]	0.31	0.07	0.30
Current ratio (Current assets/current liabilities)[b]	3.10	0.65	2.63
Cash ratio (Cash + short-term investments/current liabilities)[c]	1.83	0.26	1.56
Total assets/total liabilities[d]	1.48	0.73	1.24
Quick ratio[e] (Cash + short-term investments + accounts receivable: current liabilities)	2.09	0.46	1.74
Defensive interval ratio (days)[f] (Current assets/total expenses)	145.02	50.34	141.89

[a] A high indicator (1 and above) depicts a healthy financial position of the Agency.

[b] A high ratio (1 and above) indicates an entity's ability to pay off its short-term liabilities.

[c] A ratio below 1 is a reflection that there is insufficient cash to settle current liabilities.

[d] A high ratio (1 and above) is a good indicator of solvency.

[e] Quick ratio is a better indicator of the Agency's financial solvency, the higher the better (above 1).

[f] A favourable indicator is the number of days above 30.

18.   The overall financial ratios at the end of the financial year showed that UNRWA was able to meet its maturing current liabilities. However, the cash-to-current liabilities ratio for the programme budget, which finances core activities of the Agency, was 0.26, indicating that the Agency had insufficient cash to finance its core current liabilities as they fall due. In addition, the programme budget had current assets of only $0.65 to finance each dollar of its outstanding debt, while for quick ratio it had only $0.46 to cover immediate current liabilities, which are below the normal threshold indicator of 1.

3.   End-of-service liabilities, including after-service health insurance

19.   End-of-service liabilities, including after-service health insurance, have been growing steadily since 2012 (see table II.3), however UNRWA does not fund these obligations. At the end of 2015, UNRWA reported a liability for area staff end-of-service benefits amounting to $650.04 million, an increase of $125.50 million (24 per cent) compared with the previous year. The increase was mainly attributed to factors such as the change in percentage for calculating end-of-service liability from 11 per cent to 12 per cent of the completed years of service with effect from 2015; a revision of the discount rate from 4.75 per cent to 4.32 per cent to reflect the decrease in the interest rate for long-term United States government bonds and corporate bonds and the currency adjustment factor for the compensation of the depreciation of the United States dollar against the Israeli sheqel.

Table II.3
Trend of end-of-service liability for area staff

Year	Amount (thousands of United States dollars)	Annual increase (percentage)
2012	463 018	–
2013	491 717	6
2014	524 540	7
2015	650 035	24

Source: Note 15 to UNRWA financial statements 2015.

4. Review of financial statements

Need to revisit provision policy on VAT account receivables

20. Note 7.2 to the financial statements states that the provisions for value added tax receivable and accounts receivable are estimated amounts based on the aged analysis of the outstanding amounts as at the reporting date and those provisions have been calculated on the basis of past experience and the likelihood of collecting the outstanding amounts over the specific periods. Likewise, policy no. 16 of the Agency's financial reporting policy (para. 16) requires the Agency to take into account the risks and uncertainties that inevitably surround many events and circumstances in reaching the best estimate of a provision.

21. As of 31 December 2015 UNRWA reported gross VAT receivables of $104.61 million of which $100.60 million (96.16 per cent) was receivable from the Palestinian Authority and had been outstanding for a period ranging from 1 year to 20 years. Total provision made for doubtful VAT receivables amounted to $82.49 million of which $82.16 million (99.6 per cent) related to VAT receivable from the Palestinian Authority. The Board noted that UNRWA does not make provision for VAT receivables aged below two years despite past experience of non-recovery of VAT receivables from the Palestinian Authority.[4]

22. The Board is of the view that UNRWA needs to revise the current policy applied for the creation of provisions of doubtful debt for long outstanding VAT receivables so that VAT receivables aged from one to two years are taken into account in order for the figure reported on the financial statements to fairly present the entity's financial position on VAT receivables.

23. **UNRWA agreed with the Board's recommendation to review the policy on the creation of provisions of doubtful debt for long outstanding VAT receivables based on past experience and the likelihood of collection to reach the best estimate and fair presentation.**

5. Results-based management

Lack of midyear results review report in 2015

24. UNRWA introduced the midyear results review in 2013 to complement the established annual review process. The purpose of the results reviews is to align

---

[4] UNRWA provides 50 per cent for VAT remaining uncollected for a period of two to three years and 100 per cent for VAT outstanding for a period of more than three years.

results-based management best practices by proactively reviewing organizational performance in key areas and linking results with utilized resources. The midyear results review serves as a mechanism for executive management and other key staff to assess progress of implementation of the biennial plans, review context assumptions, update risks and approve proposed adjustments to planned achievements, review the operational environment that affects the achievement of programmatic outcomes and review the overall status of progress towards achieving the human development goals for the refugee population that UNRWA serves.

25.　However, the Board noted that UNRWA did not produce the midyear results review report for 2015, despite its importance in assessing the level of achievements and utilized financial resources, outputs, challenges encountered and the planned interventions for the subsequent six months. The Board found that the most recent results review report was issued in 2014. UNRWA attributed the non-production of the midyear results review report for 2015 to the Agency's involvement in the preparation of operational documents including the medium-term strategy for 2016-2021, together with headquarters implementation plans. UNRWA explained that it would put more emphasis on midyear reporting as a means of improving the enforcement and compliance with the planning function during the planning process in 2016.

26.　The Board noted the management initiatives but remain concerned that preparation of midyear results review reports needs priority as its absence might inhibit management from properly assessing the level of achievements, the financial resources utilized, outputs, challenges encountered and the planned interventions for the subsequent six months.

27.　**UNRWA agreed with Board's recommendation to design an action plan which will enable the midyear results review report to be issued on the due date and discussed in the results review participants meeting to support management decision-making.**

6.　Fleet management

Car log system deficiencies

28.　UNRWA introduced car log systems for its vehicles with a view to monitoring and recording vehicle fleet utilization. The system has features that maintain the vehicle fleet operations records and ultimately generate reports on fuel consumption, mileage covered and maintenance cost. The reports generated from the system are used by management for decision-making regarding fleet management. However, the Board noted the deficiencies outlined below regarding the use of the car log system, which need management intervention for further improvement and optimal use of the system.

29.　*At the Gaza field office*: The field office operates a 532-vehicle fleet with the car log system that contains a number of control devices, such as a swipe-card reader, transponder, aerial and modem to facilitate the entire system's operation. Further, the car log system has a programme which can automatically record the fuel received from the pumping system and can produce an analysis of fuel consumption. However, the existing car log system is not compatible with and does not interface with the prevailing fuel station pumping systems, which means the Agency has to use a spreadsheet to manually upload fuel consumption data into the car log system. The practice runs contrary to the intended objective of the car log system of automatic recording of fuel consumption and exposes the field office to the risk of generating incomplete reports owing to human error.

30. *At the Jordan field office*: The field office operates a 188-vehicle fleet serving headquarters in Amman and the Jordan field office and uses the car log system for its vehicle fleet. There is no service level agreement between the Information Management Services Division and the Procurement and Logistics Division to ensure the Information Management Services Division will support and maintain the car log system. The lack of such an agreement might result in failure of the car log system because the Transport and Logistics Section may not be able to provide the needed technical support to ensure that there is effective and efficient restoration of the service in case of any major malfunction of the system.

31. With respect to deficiencies noted in the Gaza field office, the Board was informed that additional soft and hard components need to be fixed both at fuel stations and in motor vehicles to make the pumping system compatible with the existing car log system. UNRWA also stated that the Information Management Services Division is currently finalizing a governance framework policy document, which is expected to be ready in the third quarter of 2016, which will have the support platform and service level agreement for all information and communications technology systems of the Procurement and Logistics Division, including the car log system.

32. UNRWA agreed with the Board's recommendation that it (a) align fuel station pumping systems with the car log system at the Gaza field office to realize the expected benefits from the system, including online capturing of vehicles' daily fuel transactions; and (b) establish a service level agreement between the Information Management Services Division and the Procurement and Logistics Division to ensure proper support of the car log system in all field offices.

7. Travel management

Lack of centralized air tickets cost management and advance ticket travel policy

33. UNRWA has established a travel management system[5] for recording and monitoring all information regarding air ticketing details, such as cost, invoice, date of travel, route, agent and type of ticket. This is a positive step towards reducing travel costs through monitoring and taking prompt action. However, the Board noted that UNRWA has not implemented the system in field offices and as a result the Agency is not capturing air ticket costs procured directly by the field offices. Instead, such information is submitted to the headquarters in a separate spreadsheet for further processing, which is prone to human error and contain inconsistencies from one field office to another.

34. For instance, the air ticket data for the year 2015 from the field office in the Syrian Arab Republic included only the booking date, the name of the airline and of the staff member, while other information required in the system[6] was missing.

---

[5] Installed as a pilot at headquarters in Amman.

[6] The data for the field office in the Syrian Arab Republic did not disclose the air ticket cost, ticket number and invoice number.

UNRWA stated that the initiative is in progress to roll out the system to the field offices by 2016.

35. In addition, the Board found that UNRWA did not have an advance ticket travel purchase policy, which ultimately resulted in most tickets being booked only a short time before the dates of travel. For example, the Board found that bookings for 222 (58 per cent) air tickets, amounting to $114,688, out of 383 sampled air tickets, were made between 1 and 5 days before the dates of travel, when ticket prices are likely to be higher than those for bookings made in advance.[7] While UNRWA attributed this deficiency to the long internal process for approving travel, the Board considers that the key problem is the lack of documented advance ticket booking policy to guide and streamline travel management approval processes.

36. UNRWA agreed with the Board's recommendation that it (a) expedite the roll-out process for the travel management system in field offices, to strengthen efficient recording and monitoring of air travel costs and enhance consistency in recording air ticket information; (b) develop a travel management policy which will define the air ticket booking arrangement; and (c) streamline the approval processes with regard to the travel management system so that they are completed within a reasonable time.

8. Procurement and contract management

Motor vehicle insurance contract management

37. UNRWA entered into a contract on 6 November 2013 for insuring 1,472 Agency vehicles (at a cost of $632,960), which ended on 31 August 2014. According to article 3.1 of the contract, the contract should be effective upon signature notwithstanding a possible later effective date.

38. UNRWA renewed the contract from November 2014 to August 2015 and then from 1 September 2015 to 31 August 2016. The Board found that in both cases, the renewal was neither done through competitive tendering nor preceded by the evaluation of the vendor's performance as required under chapter 12.4 of the UNRWA procurement manual (2012). Further, the contract was signed on 14 October 2015, despite the expiration of the previous contract since 31 August 2015, representing a delay of 44 days. In addition, the performance security, equivalent to 20 per cent of the premium paid, was submitted on 29 October 2015, after the extension of the contract, contrary to the requirement of article 1.1.20 of the contract which requires the performance security to be submitted prior to signing of the contract.

39. The Board is concerned that the late signing of the contract might weaken the entity's legal position in cases of contractual disputes (the Agency might not be compensated in case the insured motor vehicles are damaged or stolen) and delayed submission of the performance security increases the possibility of losing monetary compensation in case of dispute/default from the service provider. The Board also considers that the entity cannot optimize the use of procurement resources by obtaining the most economical rates and the best terms under the contract due to the absence of competitive tendering.

---

[7] According to research by Carlson Wagonlit Travel (CWT) Travel Management Institute (2007), tickets purchased 14 days in advance might cost 50 per cent less than a ticket purchased 3 days or fewer from the date of departure.

40.   **UNRWA agreed with the Board's recommendation that it ensure: (a) the timely signing of the insurance contract before its expiration; (b) that all future insurance contract extensions are preceded by an evaluation of the supplier as required under chapter 12.4 of the UNRWA procurement manual (2012); and (c) the conduct of competitive tendering in 2016 so as to obtain competitive terms and price for the insurance of motor vehicles.**

Non-provision of feedback to unsuccessful suppliers

41.   Chapter 9.3.1.1 of the UNRWA procurement manual (2012) requires unsuccessful suppliers to be informed in writing for all contracts above $100,000 and the information regarding contracts awarded to be uploaded onto the Agency's website. However, from the review of seven contracts worth $3.27 million, the Board found no documented evidence to confirm feedback had been provided to unsuccessful bidders as required by the procurement manual.

42.   The Board was informed that feedback was not often communicated by the Transport and Logistics Section to unsuccessful suppliers, owing to a shortage of staff and the heavy workload facing the section. Further, UNRWA explained that, in 2016, the Agency had implemented electronic tendering software (In-Tend), which includes automated feedback to both successful and unsuccessful bidders. The new system will scale up to include all new procurement and contracts for headquarters in Amman, with a plan to include all field offices in the fourth quarter of 2016 and the first quarter of 2017.

43.   The Board is of the view that the lack of feedback to unsuccessful suppliers may affect the reputation of the Agency on fair evaluation and limit the level of transparency in the procurement process. The deficiency also reduces the confidence of bidders in applying for future tenders and affect the level of competition.

44.   **The Board recommends that UNRWA expedite the implementation of the electronic tendering software in all field offices and headquarters to ensure feedback is issued and communicated to unsuccessful suppliers, in order to enhance transparency in the procurement process.**

Inadequate justification of waivers

45.   Chapter 5.4.1 (paras. 1 and 3) of the UNRWA procurement manual (2012) provides circumstances where waivers in the competitive procurement process are acceptable and if the waiver is necessary, the justification should be properly recorded for future reference. The Board sampled 10 out of 17 tender files of waivers authorized to shorten the tender periods to expedite the procurement process at the Gaza field office (representing a cost of $3.18 million). The Board noted that of the 10 waivers, only 2 (20 per cent), valued at $1.76 million, were supported by acceptable reasons, while the reasons given for the remaining 8 waivers (80 per cent) were mainly attributed to delays by the user departments in raising lists of requirements and in placing orders. The Board considers that granting waivers for costs which amounted to $1.42 million, without justifiable reasons, highlights a deficiency in planning and the lack of regular review of inventory balance to ensure that the replenishment of supplies is done in a timely manner, so as to avoid emergency procurement and avoidable waivers.

46.   The Board was informed that UNRWA had taken steps, such as preparing a consolidated procurement plan, making the preparation of the plan a mandatory requirement and establishing over 75 long-term agreements. UNRWA believes that the measures taken will ensure that all procurement requirements are identified in a timely manner and communicated to the Procurement and Logistics Division to avoid unnecessary shortening of tender periods.

47.   The Board is of the view that shortening tender periods might lead to low vendor response and participation owing to the insufficient time given for the preparation and submission of a tender. It also limits the scope of competition among vendors and might eventually have an impact on the tender price.

48.   In addition, the Gaza field office had 16 long-term agreements with different suppliers, who provide the most frequently procured items or services over a specific period of time. However, five (63 per cent) of the agreements were extended without performance evaluation of the suppliers, contrary to chapter 12.4 of the UNRWA procurement manual (2012).

49.   UNRWA stated that the evaluation had not been performed because there were no reports from end users of weak performance by the suppliers. Nevertheless, the Board considers that the field performance evaluation needs to be proactive rather than reactive, so as to improve the performance of suppliers. Extending the contract without an evaluation of suppliers' performance exposes the Agency to the risk of engaging suppliers with unsatisfactory performance.

50.   **UNRWA agreed with the Board's recommendation that it (a) strengthen coordination between procurement and user departments to ensure that all procurement requirements are identified in a timely manner and communicated to Procurement and Logistics Division to avoid unnecessary shortening of the tender period; and (b) ensure the Gaza field office performs an evaluation of suppliers' performance prior to the extension of long-term agreements and use the evaluation report as criteria for such extensions.**

Delays in the delivery of goods and services

51.   The Board reviewed 16 purchase orders, amounting to $6 million, at the Gaza field office, and noted that the deliveries of goods and services for 7 of the purchase orders (44 per cent), worth $2.69 million, were completed after delays, ranging from 30 days to 110 days from contractual due dates, but that no liquidated damages were imposed upon the suppliers for late deliveries. The Board is concerned that the delays might affect the service delivery levels expected for the Palestine refugees. UNRWA attributed the delays to restrictions at the borders of the host countries, with the exception of few cases where the delays resulted from the vendors' fault. The Board was informed that the Gaza field office is trying to provide all necessary assistance to vendors in cases where they face restrictions that require the involvement of management and currently the Agency is considering establishing a new coordination mechanism for UNRWA goods with the Israeli side through the Coordination of Government Activities in the Territories department.

52.   The Board acknowledges the challenges faced by the Agency, but still considers that the end user and procurement departments need to work together for close follow-up and to improve coordination with suppliers for the delays caused by the suppliers. In addition, while UNRWA stated that liquidated damages are part of

general conditions of contracts attached to all purchase orders to suppliers, the Board found no evidence of their enforcement at the Gaza field office. Therefore, the Board considers that UNRWA needs to include a specific clause for liquidated damages for the delays caused by the suppliers.

53. UNRWA agreed with the Board's recommendation that it (a) strengthen the Contract Management Unit to improve the level of follow-up with the vendors to minimize delays in the delivery of goods and services; (b) ensure specific liquidated damages clauses are included in the contract and/or purchase orders; and (c) consider establishing a new coordination mechanism for UNRWA goods with the Israeli side through the Coordination of Government Activities in the Territories department.

Inadequate internal controls over vendor suspension process

54. Chapter 4.4.1, subparagraphs (a) to (h) of the procurement manual (2012) provides the basis for striking off the vendor in cases of default on the terms and conditions of the contracts. In addition, chapter 4.4.1.2 of the manual requires the recommendation to declare a supplier as ineligible, or to remove or suspend a supplier from the UNRWA vendors' list, to be coordinated with the Legal Adviser and General Counsel and the Director of Administrative Support before it is communicated to the suppliers.

55. The Board examined vendor suspension processes at the Gaza field office and noted that four vendors were suspended but that the suspension was decided upon by the Head of Procurement in the field office without coordination with the Legal Adviser and General Counsel and the Director of Administrative Support, as required under chapter 4.4.1.2 of the UNRWA procurement manual (2012). Further, the Board noted the sanctions and complaints committee at headquarters in Amman has not been established, contrary to paragraph 3.3.3 of the new procurement manual (third version of the manual, 2015).

56. The Board is of the view that the suspension of vendors without following proper procedures might reduce the credibility of the Agency and suppliers' confidence towards the Agency. In addition, the Agency needs to establish the sanction and complaints committee to handle the sanctioning of vendors in a transparent and fair manner.

57. UNRWA agreed with the Board's recommendation that it (a) establish the sanction and complaints committee to handle the sanctioning of vendors in a transparent and fair manner; and (b) ensure suspension procedures, such as coordination with the Legal Adviser and General Counsel and the Director of Administrative Support, are adhered to.

9. Human resource management

Inadequate management of individual consultants and contractors

58. Organizational directive No. 29 requires the hiring director to conduct performance evaluation of individual consultants and contractors in order to provide assurance on the quality of service delivered. The Board's review of contracts and consultants' records from different hiring departments revealed the findings outlined below.

59. Evaluation was not performed for 15 out of 16 contracts of consultants and contractors (94 per cent), from different hiring departments at headquarters in Amman. In addition, 10 hiring departments did not maintain individual consultants' files, despite their importance in keeping track of all correspondence between UNRWA headquarters in Amman and the consultants. Likewise, performance evaluation was not conducted for 5 out of 15 consultants and contractors (33 per cent), from different hiring departments at the Jordan field office.

60. The Board considers that the noted deficiencies are mainly owing to the lack of a documented policy to formalize the process of evaluating individual consultants and contractors. UNRWA stated that it will remind the hiring departments of the provisions of paragraph 70 of organizational directive No. 29, particularly regarding their responsibility to keep records (files) for consultants and contractors, and will establish a uniform approach in performance evaluation during the ongoing revision of the Agency's policy on the hiring of consultants and contractors.

61. The Board is of the view that, without performance evaluation as a reliable basis for assessing performance, it will be difficult to determine whether the established needs and objectives that led to the engagement of the consultants and contractors were achieved. It also limits the tracking of historical performance of previously engaged consultants and contractors for future engagement.

62. Further, the Board noted that the terms of reference for hiring individual consultants and contractors at UNRWA headquarters in Amman and the Jordan field office do not include measurable outputs of the assigned task, such as objectives, targets and performance indicators, as a baseline against which to evaluate contractors and consultants' performance. This is contrary to the requirement of paragraph 17 of organizational directive No. 29 and it may affect the effectiveness of the performance appraisal of individual consultants and contractors.

63. **UNRWA agreed with the Board's recommendation that it (a) conduct performance evaluation and keep records for the engaged consultants and contractors; (b) expedite the process of policy review to formalize the performance evaluation of individual consultants and contractors; and (c) ensure all hiring departments include measurable outputs and performance indicators in their terms of reference for the monitoring and evaluation of results.**

Long outstanding salary advances

64. From the review of the aging schedule of salary advances in the field office in the Syrian Arab Republic for three consecutive years (2012 to 2014), the Board noted cases where salary advances had been outstanding for periods ranging from 12 to 36 months. This is contrary to part 1.3 of the Policy, which requires salary advances made pursuant to Area Staff Rule 103.4.1 (f) to be recovered within 12 consecutive equal monthly payments commencing in the month after the advance is granted to a staff member. UNRWA stated that the long outstanding salary advances relate to staff members who are on special leave without pay and the balance ($56,030)[8] will remain outstanding until the end of their leave. However, the Board considers that the long outstanding salary advance is mainly owing to the existing gap in the current salary advance policy, which is silent on the clearance

---

[8] 2012: $632, 2013: $8,522, 2014: $46,876.

procedures for outstanding salary advances, in the case where staff members are on special leave without pay.

65. The Board recommends UNRWA review the policy to ensure that procedures for releasing staff for special leave without pay take into account clearance of the outstanding salary advances.

10. Health programme management

Management of pharmaceutical supplies at Gaza field office

66.   Annex 9 to the report of the World Health Organization Expert Committee on Specifications for Pharmaceutical Preparations (WHO Technical Report Series, No. 908, 2003) outlines the requirements for the premises and facilities used for the storage of pharmaceutical supplies to be prepared with precautions so as to prevent unauthorized persons from entering the storage areas. However, the Board noted that the general store in the Gaza field office is accessible by officers who are not responsible for pharmaceutical supplies. This highlights inadequate access control and is contrary to good storage practice as stipulated in the report of the Expert Committee. In addition, the general store had no temperature regulators for drugs in need of a certain level of temperature (antibiotic suspensions, capsules, syrups, multivitamin drops and tablets, creams and ointments) for proper storage conditions. For example, during the Board's visit, the actual temperature in the store was 26°C against the required temperatures of 15°C to 25°C.

67.   The Board considers that it is crucial for the field office to abide by good storage practices for pharmaceuticals defined by the World Health Organization Expert Committee so as to ensure that quality of medicine and medical supplies is maintained.

68.   UNRWA agreed with the Board's recommendation that it (a) establish a separate store for medical supplies in the new building, to avoid mixing them with general supplies; and (b) install temperature regulators in the general store to facilitate proper drugs storage management.

Frequent stock-out cases

69.   The Board found frequent stock-out cases at the Gaza field office. For example, 48 drug items were out of stock for a period ranging from 35 days to 509 days, including crucial drug items such as Amlodipine tablets, which ran out of stock for 140 days, and Fluconazole capsules, which were out of stock for 293 days. UNRWA attributed the stock-out cases to unrest and the emergency situation in Gaza and stock delivery delays. UNRWA explained that it has recently established a strategic approach for the procurement of medicines and the creation of a buffer stock to avoid such stock outs. Also the use of the enterprise resource planning system in managing stock will create a normal routine system for determining stock levels and reorder points.

70.   The Board considers that there is insufficient follow-up with the Procurement and Logistics Division to ensure the steady availability of essential drugs through the establishment of a sufficient buffer stock, given the critical political unrest in which the Gaza field office operates.

71. **UNRWA agreed with the Board's recommendation that it establish buffer stock to ensure efficient operations and to meet the minimum operational requirements for unexpected emergencies in field offices.**

11. Programme and project management

Camp improvement pilot project at Deir El-Balah camp

72. In 2015, UNRWA entered into an agreement with a contractor for the reconstruction of Deir El-Balah camp, with a contract sum of $40 million for a period of 30 months from 21 January 2015 to 21 July 2017.

73. Based on the project implementation milestones, there were substantial delays in some of the pre-implementation activities, such as completion of urban planning, conducting interviews with beneficiaries for demolishing their houses and rebuilding new residences. The activities were planned to be implemented in August 2015 but had not been implemented as at the time of the Board's visit in April 2016.

74. In addition, the draft removal analysis showed that the Agency had neither budgeted nor included the cost of rental services[9] in respect of the temporary transfer of families to allow camp reconstruction.

75. UNRWA attributed the project implementation delays to the delays in the review of the project master plan by a consultant, who was updating it by incorporating the input from thematic workshops. In addition, UNRWA explained that some families opposed the project, which forced the Agency to look for other options, including appointing a team to conduct some "vertical densification" within the camp borders to find acceptable solutions. While the Board acknowledges the initiatives undertaken to implement the project, it considers that the severe delays encountered to date jeopardize the successful delivery of the project on time and within budget. In future, UNRWA needs to conduct risk analysis, sensitization initiatives and adequate budgetary estimates before any project implementation process.

76. **UNRWA agreed with the Board's recommendation that it (a) expedite the process of finalizing the master plan by incorporating all risks and concerns of the beneficiaries to allow smooth project implementation; (b) conduct sensitization of the affected households as part of an awareness-raising exercise regarding the benefits of the project; (c) expedite the vertical densification study and incorporate the results into the project master plan; and (d) finalize the transfer budget estimates for the temporary renting of accommodation for the families whose shelter will be demolished prior to their transfer to new residences.**

12. Information and communications technology

Lack of information and communications technology strategy

77. UNRWA planning processes require the development of the six-year medium-term strategy, which shows strategic outcomes for the Agency as well as the two-year implementation plans for the field offices and headquarters. High-level business objectives and requirements for information system division are outlined

---

[9] Temporary transfer of families involves the cost of rental to keep the families in a temporary new residence.

under the Department of Administrative Support while the task of identification of the projects to be executed based on high-level requirements of the headquarters implementation plan is left under the responsibility of the Information Management Services Division.

78. The review of the medium-term strategy (2010-2015) and pertinent implementation plan (2014-2015) revealed that UNRWA does not have an information and communications technology strategy for identifying the information and communications technology vision, mission and objectives together with the targeted enterprise architecture and road map to achieve it. The absence of a strategic plan in this regard exposes the Agency to the risk of delays in building up information and communications technology capabilities required to support its strategic intentions and for responding in a timely manner to organizational transformation.

79. UNRWA stated that its focus for the past three years was on the implementation of the enterprise resource plan and therefore an information and communications technology strategy was not developed. It would ensure that, through the implementation of new organizational directive No. 26 on information and communications technology the strategy would be developed in 2016.

80. **UNRWA agreed with the Board's recommendation to develop an information and communications technology strategy together with enterprise architecture and road map to support the Agency's business objectives.**

Lack of information technology applications portfolio management framework

81. Information technology application portfolio management is a framework for managing enterprise information technology software applications and software-based services which provides managers with an inventory of the company's software applications and metrics to illustrate the business benefits of each application.

82. In UNRWA, an enterprise information technology application is defined in the register as an information technology application whose service was intended to be offered to all five field offices of operation and is administered and maintained by the Information Management Services Division at headquarters. According to the register of all enterprise information technology applications, UNRWA had a total of 30 information technology applications managed by the Division, consisting of seven externally acquired and 23 internally developed applications (see table II.4).

Table II.4
Summary of information technology applications

Department	Number of information technology applications
Administrative Support Services	11
Education	4
Health department	2
Human resources	8
Infrastructure and camp improvement	2
Microfinance	1
Provident fund	1
Relief and social services	1

Source: UNRWA data.

83.   From the review of the register of information technology applications, the Board noted the following deficiencies, which might have an impact on the management of the information technology applications portfolio within the Agency:

(a)   There are information technology applications under other departments, such as the enterprise resource planning system, which are not included in the register of information technology applications;

(b)   UNRWA was unable to provide metrics to illustrate the business benefits of each information technology application in use at the Agency;

(c)   As a result of the distribution of hosting and responsibility for information technology applications among various Agency departments, the solution architectures for those departments have duplicate applications. For example, the Administrative Support Department had three applications for inventory management, namely, the inventory system used by the Information Management Services Division, a service inventory system and a barcode system;

(d)   The time taken to roll out applications within the Agency is longer than normal. For example, an e-health application commissioned in 2009 was operating in only four field offices as at the time of final audit (April 2016), equivalent to 80 per cent roll-out accomplished in six years.

84.   The Board considers that the deficiencies were mainly owing to the lack of an information technology application portfolio management framework for recording and monitoring the inventory of the Agency's software applications and metrics to illustrate the business benefit of each application. The framework would also facilitate the evaluation of applications based on factors such as cost, risk and business value, and determine where to continue investment and where to reduce and consolidate. The Board was informed that an information technology application portfolio management framework will come as part of creating the overall information technology governance management framework as stipulated in the revised organizational directive No. 26 on information systems. However, the time frame for developing the framework was not stated.

85. **The Board recommends that UNRWA expedite the process of developing and implementing an information technology applications portfolio management framework for the proper management of the Agency's software applications.**

Lack of the benefits realization plan for the enterprise resource planning project

86. In its report for 2013 (A/69/5/Add.4, para. 155) the Board recommended that UNRWA develop a benefits realization plan for the enterprise resource planning project and integrate it with the project master plan to ensure effective monitoring and the realization of benefits. The benefits realization plan is a vital document that outlines the expected benefits from the new enterprise resource planning project and details how such benefits would be measured, including who is accountable for such measurement and when.

87. However, at the time of the final audit (March-April 2016), the Board found that a benefits realization plan had not been developed. The Board considers that it is crucial that a comprehensive benefits realization plan is developed to guide management in ensuring that the identified benefits are monitored and opportunities expected from the project are realized at an optimal level.

88. While the Board appreciates that the Agency has developed potential operational and technology opportunities and that it is in the process of adopting and implementing a benefits realization plan for the enterprise resource planning project, it remains concerned that it has taken too long to develop the plan.

89. **The Board reiterates its previous recommendation that UNRWA expedite the development of a benefits realization plan for the enterprise resource planning project to ensure effective monitoring and the realization of the intended benefits.**

Enterprise resource planning project post-implementation review

90. UNRWA introduced a new enterprise resource planning system to respond to the need for an integrated system that fully supports the needs of the Agency and enables the effective management of human, financial and physical resources. The new enterprise resource planning system was also necessary as the supplier of the previous system (Ramco) expected to cease supporting the system after 2014. After multiple extensions, including delays in delivery for phases I and II of the project, which were expected to go live in June 2014 and January 2015 respectively, the system ultimately went live successfully in April 2015, at the final cost of $32.66 million, slightly exceeding the cost estimate of $29.51 million.

91. After the launch of the project, a post-implementation review is a crucial step in project implementation to evaluate whether project objectives were met; determine how effectively the project was run; learn lessons for the future; and ensure that the Agency gets the greatest possible benefit from the project.

92. UNRWA planned to complete a post-implementation evaluation for the project by November 2015, but the evaluation was not conducted. The Board was informed that the evaluation was cancelled owing to lack of capacity and competing priorities. The Board believes that a thorough and timely post-implementation review is crucial for the Agency to identify key lessons learned, scope for improvement and for proper planning and management of future projects.

93. **The Board recommends that UNRWA conduct a post-implementation review of the enterprise resource planning project to identify key lessons learned for improvement in future projects.**

Lack of transition plan for technical maintenance of the enterprise resource planning system

94. According to organizational directive No. 26, the Chief of the Technology Services Division is responsible for designing, developing, implementing and managing the Agency enterprise information and communications technology infrastructure and services, including service desk support.

95. Since the introduction of the enterprise resource planning system, the contractor of the system had the responsibility for technical and application management until 31 December 2015. The Agency's contract with the contractor was extended from 1 January 2016 to 31 March 2016 and then from 1 April 2016 to 30 June 2016. Nevertheless, UNRWA did not have a transition plan and did not conduct training to transfer knowledge and build internal capacity for technical and application management of the enterprise resource planning system. The Board is concerned that the short-term view taken by UNRWA in handling the system, such as offering three-month contract extensions and the lack of transition plan for developing capability, may affect the ability of the Agency to maintain the smooth operation of the system over the long term.

96. **The Board recommends that UNRWA prepare a transition plan to develop the internal capacity needed to manage key technical and application activities.**

97. UNRWA notified the Board that it has awarded a three-year contract for service support for the SAP enterprise resource planning system and that recruitment of a staff member for SAP support is under way.

Lack of interface between the enterprise resource planning system and e-Health

98. UNRWA implementation of e-Health started in 2009 with the classic e-Health version being implemented in the Jordan, Lebanon and Gaza field offices, followed by another version for the Family Health Team in 2013. Currently, the classic e-Health package is fully implemented in 59 out of 143 health centres (41 per cent).

99. However, the Board noted that the new the enterprise resource planning system, which is the main system in UNRWA, does not interface with the e-Health system at the health centres. Currently, UNRWA uses a spreadsheet for the preparation of stock consumption reports, which are conducted quarterly after stocktaking and the data are uploaded in the enterprise resource planning system. Interface between the two systems is necessary to facilitate the exchange of information between the health centres and the main warehouse.

100. The lack of interface between the two systems requires human intervention and increases the risk of stock misstatement owing to human error. It also causes difficulties in ascertaining the daily stock consumption at the level of the health centres.

101. The Board considers that the full implementation of the e-Health application will improve the visibility of pharmacy stock levels and ultimately enhance a real-time recording of consumption at the level of the health centres, increase

accountability and efficiency through the current enterprise resource planning system and eventually improve the overall financial reporting process. While UNRWA stated that it was reviewing the roll-out plan of e-Health to speed up its implementation, no definite date for completion of the roll-out of e-Health has been set.

102. The Board recommends that UNRWA (a) expedite the implementation of the e-Health application to all health centres to enable real-time recording of stock consumptions at the level of health centres; and (b) implement the interface between the e-Health application and the enterprise resource planning system to improve the quality of the financial reporting process for inventory.

Insufficient technical instructions

103. In its previous report (A/70/5/Add.4, para. 93), the Board recommended that UNRWA review the backup policy and procedure for user access to reflect the new requirements of the enterprise resource planning system. During the current audit, the Board noted that the 2014 backup policy and the 2012 access control policy provide adequate controls coverage to include the new system. However, contrary to paragraph 5.7.4 of the information security policy, the Agency had no clearly defined and documented procedure to guide the provision, change and closing of users' accounts, nor a procedure for creating, changing and deleting roles in the system.

104. The Board is of the view that the absence of procedures guiding the provision and suspension of user access increases the risk of granting inappropriate user access rights.

105. UNRWA agreed with the Board's recommendation that procedures to define and document the provision and suspension of user access for the enterprise resource planning system be developed, as well as for the creation, change and deletion of roles in the system.

Non-compliance with technical instructions

106. The information and communications technology infrastructure guidelines and standards for remote sites (technical instruction No. 10) is a technical instruction outlining the compliance requirements with respect to the quality of service for remote area network connectivity, to ensure stable and consistent connectivity performance when the network is overloaded. UNRWA needs quality network connectivity because it operates from five different locations, namely Jordan, Gaza, the West Bank, Lebanon and the Syrian Arab Republic, which are supported by enterprise systems. However, the Board noted that UNRWA does not have information technology tools that can be used to monitor the quality of service metrics stated in the technical instructions and that the compliance review regarding network connectivity has not yet been conducted.

107. The Board is of the view that the lack of visibility with respect to the quality of service for network connectivity at UNRWA may cause all the enterprise systems running within the Agency network not to perform at an acceptable level.

108. UNRWA agreed with the Board's recommendation that it (a) acquire information technology tools for monitoring the quality of network service in accordance with technical instruction No. 10; and (b) perform regular

monitoring of the quality of service metrics to ensure stable network connectivity.

Information and communications technology security governance

109. According to the Agency's organizational directive No. 26 (October 2015) the Commissioner-General delegates information and communications technology responsibilities to the Deputy Commissioner-General. In managing the information and communications technology operations, the Deputy Commissioner-General establishes and chairs the information and communications technology governance board to support, review and undertake decision-making responsibilities, such as endorsing information and communications technology goals and strategy, establishing steering committees and monitoring of information and communications technology performance.

110. During its audit, the Board found that the steering committee for information and communications technology had not been established and security responsibilities were spread among various information and communications technology personnel, rather than being centralized to information and communications technology security personnel to get the needed focus in discharging activities of the information security programme. This is against section 12.4 of UNRWA organizational directive No. 26, which requires the Agency to establish and maintain a framework to guide the development and maintenance of a comprehensive information security programme in accordance with the information security policy.

111. In addition, the Board found that there is no committee accountable for ensuring that information security strategies are aligned with and support business objectives. The Board noted that the information security policy in force, created in February 2011, was out of date and still included references to a defunct committee.

112. The Board is of the view that the absence of a framework to guide the development and maintenance of a comprehensive information security programme, the absence of an information security steering committee and the lack of an updated information security policy may compromise the Agency's ability to protect itself from information security risks.

113. UNRWA explained that it had established the Information and Communications Technology Board, which will be requested to establish a security steering committee. Furthermore, the Agency was in the process of hiring an information security officer.

114. **UNRWA agreed with the Board's recommendation that it (a) develop a comprehensive information security programme; (b) update its information security policy; and (c) develop an information security steering committee and assign accountability to ensure information security strategies are aligned with and support business objectives.**

13. Department of Internal Oversight Services

Overall performance of the Department of Internal Oversight Services for the year ended 2015

115. The Board review noted that, over a period of four years (from January 2012 to December 2015) the Department of Internal Oversight Services issued a total of

402 audit recommendations, of which 298 (74 per cent) were fully implemented, 43 (11 per cent) were partially implemented and 61 (15 per cent) had not been implemented as at 31 December 2015 (see table II.5). In comparison with the status of implementation of 530 recommendations issued in the four years to 31 December 2014, 455 (86 per cent) were fully implemented, 39 (7 per cent) were partially implemented, while 36 (7 per cent) were not implemented.

Table II.5
Status of implementation of recommendations issued by the Department of Internal Oversight Services

	Year of issue					
Status as at 31 December	2012	2013	2014	2015	Total	Percentage
Not implemented	–	16	15	30	61	15
Partially implemented (in progress)	2	23	12	6	43	11
Fully implemented	141	117	22	18	298	74
Total	**143**	**156**	**49**	**54**	**402**	**100**

Source: Department of Internal Oversight Services tracking sheet, April 2016.

116. The rate of implementation of general recommendations made by the Department of Internal Oversight Services had declined by 12 per cent, from 86 per cent for the four-year period ended 2014, to 74 per cent for the four-year period ended 2015.

117. The Board also noted that of 128 high-risk recommendations issued from 2012 to 2015, 105 (82 per cent) had been fully implemented, while 9 (7 per cent) were partially implemented and 14 (11 per cent) were not implemented (see table II.6).

Table II.6
Trend of outstanding high-risk recommendations from 2012-2015

	Year of issue					
Status as at 31 December	2012	2013	2014	2015	Total	Percentage
Not implemented	–	4	5	5	14	11
Partially implemented	–	5	4	–	9	7
Fully implemented (closed)	52	35	7	11	105	82
Total	**52**	**44**	**16**	**16**	**128**	**100**

Source: Department of Internal Oversight Services tracking sheet, April 2016.

118. Despite the Agency's efforts to implement the high-risk recommendations, the Board considers that there is scope for improvement to clear the 14 outstanding high-risk recommendations so as to improve internal control systems and avoid similar deficiencies in future.

119. **The Board recommends that UNRWA continue to improve the noted internal control deficiencies by expediting the implementation of Department**

of Internal Oversight Services recommendations, especially the high-risk recommendations.

14. Microfinance Department

120. The Microfinance Department is a small programme within UNRWA that provides credit facilities to micro-entrepreneurs. The activities and balances of the Department for 2015 have been included in the Agency's financial statements for 2015. The Department prepares its own set of financial statements under the International Financial Reporting Standards, which are audited separately by the Board.

121. In 2015, the Department recorded a surplus of $0.408 million, compared with a loss of $0.484 million in 2014. The recorded surplus resulted from: an increase in interest on loans and training income; a decrease in provision expenses for impaired loans, from $1.05 million in 2014 to $0.70 million in 2015; and a decrease in some of its operating expenses. The Board audited the 2015 annual financial statements and issued an unqualified opinion.

Management of loans receivable

122. The Board reviewed the loans receivable and noted that loans amounting to $37.89 million were issued in 2015 (2014: $34.38 million) while $34.74 million (2014: $30.74 million) was received as repayment on outstanding loans. Provisions on outstanding loans as at 31 December 2015 was $0.70 million (2014: $1.05 million) while the amount of loans written off was $0.80 million (2014: $0.86 million). The closing loan balance as at 31 December 2015 was $23.83 million (2014: $21.37 million).

123. As in its previous audit report (A/70/5/Add.4, chap. II, para. 112) the Board continues to note deficiencies in the implementation of the internal auditor's recommendations concerning the deficiencies in the process of granting loans which may eventually increase the loan recoverability risk. The noted deficiencies relate to inaccuracy and inconsistency by loan officers in filling out application forms; non-compliance with loan operating manuals and non-adherence to procedures related to cashier functions; inadequate follow-up of late and delinquent clients by branch officials; and inadequate project supervision and monitoring by the branch officials as stipulated in the terms and conditions of the disbursed loans. Examples of the weaknesses noted in 2015 are as follows:

(a) At Al Bayader Branch, the cashier does not perform spot checks on temporary cash receipt books, does not sign the last temporary cash receipt used by the loan officer, there is no evidence that the remaining temporary cash receipt is checked by the cashier to ensure that no temporary cash receipts are missing and that three copies of the temporary cash receipt book are maintained. This is contrary to the Microfinance Department operating manual, which requires the cashier to perform spot checks and the loan officer to sign temporary cash receipt books and maintain three copies of the temporary cash receipt book;

(b) There were no cashier's notes in clients' files to reflect the payments collected, legal fees, stamped cheques and other matters. Most of the cheques or promissory notes relating to the closed loans are not stamped as cancelled and the reasons for cancellation are not documented by the cashier on the cancelled cash receipts in order to be reviewed by the Branch Manager prior to approval. There was also a lack of segregation of duties in some activities, for instance the cashier receives the payments from clients, creates cash receipts in the system and the system allows the cashier to cancel the cash receipts;

(c)   There were cases whereby, as a result of an oversight, weak credit decisions were rendered by branches. For instance, at Jenin branch they granted a loan of 6,000 Jordanian dinar ($8,475) to a client without the Credit Operations Manager having conducted a site visit, as required by the operating manual. In addition, the history of the clients or guarantor and their obligations were not appropriately analysed, which may increase the risk of defaulting.

124. The Board is of the view that the noted deficiencies are the result of inadequate regular training being provided to cashiers, which leaves them unable to strictly comply with Microfinance Department operating manuals and procedures related to the cashier's functions as well as the workload handled by them.

125. The Board recommends that the Microfinance Department (a) ensure verification officers monitor the application controls related to cashier functions and address issues of non-compliance to Department management on a regular basis; (b) reallocate the function of cancelling cash-received vouchers to a person other than the cashier, so as to ensure proper segregation of duties; (c) make sure that full justification for the cancellation reasons are preapproved by the branch manager and documented for future reference; and (d) ensure that full and detailed information and analysis are obtained and made for both client and guarantor.

126. The Board reiterates its previous recommendation that the Microfinance Department (a) review and strengthen the loan granting process to ensure that operating manuals and established policies and procedures are followed in filling the loan applications, in order to improve accuracy and consistency; (b) monitor the controls related to cashier functions and address non-compliance issues on a regular basis; (c) ensure proper maintenance of customers' files where all customers' guarantees and related documents are kept and updated; (d) improve project follow-up procedures (supervision and monitoring) to reduce risks of incorrect acceptance of credit decisions and decrease the risk of client default; and (e) ensure adherence to credit terms and conditions before the disbursement of loans.

Information system

127. The Board reviewed the loan management information system (Omni application), which computerizes all operational aspects of loan products currently offered by the Microfinance Department and identified the following control weaknesses, which require management intervention:

- *Unauthorized user access privileges*: The access control to the system requires the application owner to authorize the nature and extent of user access privileges, and such privileges to be periodically reviewed by the application owner to verify the access privileges. On the Omni application, the system administrator is responsible for assigning access privileges to new users in accordance with a request form, which includes the employee's job title and field management approval. From a sample of 26 new employees from different field offices, the Board found that 14 of the new employees (54 per cent) were granted access to the system without following the application procedures, as there were neither completed application forms nor approval by their senior manager prior to access being granting by the system administrator. The ad hoc provision of access to the Omni application increases the risk of inappropriate access.

128. **The Microfinance Department agreed with the Board's recommendation that the existing UNRWA user access forms be used to capture access requests in order to facilitate a clear understanding of user access requirements and document formal supervisor/manager approvals of requests for the audit trail and future reference.**

  • *Monitoring of privilege access*: The access control to the system requires the use of privileged access ("super user") on the domain and applications to be granted to appropriate personnel and logged and reviewed by management. However, the Board noted[10] that no formal reviews were being performed of the access logs and event viewer to detect any discrepancies in accessing the active directory, application and database through privileged accounts. In addition, the Board noted that the entity does not have controls, such as an independent security department, which monitors the access logs and records the activities for the high privilege and sensitive accounts in order to ensure no occurrence of violations of any type. Furthermore, the Board found that there are no access logs and formal procedures in place to review the activities performed by the administrator role on all access levels (domain, network, system software and applications) and that the passwords for these administrator accounts are not properly recorded to support the succession plan. The lack of procedures to review activities of super user accounts weakens the monitoring of these high privilege accounts and increases the risk of losing data integrity through unauthorized activities.

129. **The Microfinance Department agreed with the Board's recommendation that it (a) maintain an audit trail (logs) and monitor the actions of such sensitive user accounts and sign off on a periodic basis by an information security officer or a person with similar responsibilities who is independent from the information technology team; and (b) define and formally document administrator accounts on all levels and the passwords for the administrator accounts must be properly secured and kept with the agency's management, with access to be granted through a formal process.**

  • *Password standard on SQL database*: The access control to the system requires the identity of users (both local and remote) to be authenticated to the application systems, databases, network and communication software, and systems software through passwords or other authentication mechanisms, in compliance with entity security policies. The use of passwords incorporates policies on periodic change, confidentiality and password format (e.g., password length, alphanumeric content). The Board noted that access control over the domain active directory, Omni application and database was ineffective since the password complexity, lockout and password expiration

---

[10] From Microfinance Department internal audit report for the year ended 31 December 2015.

requirements are disabled. The noted deficiency may weaken the built-in security in the database management system.

130. The Microfinance Department agreed with the Board's recommendation that password standards be strengthened on the SQL database for the Omni application so as to conform with best practices by enforcing password complexity, lockout and expiration requirements.

C. Disclosures by management

131. UNRWA made the following disclosures relating to write-offs, ex gratia payments and cases of fraud and presumptive fraud, which in the view of the Board are not significant.

1. Write-off of losses of cash, receivables and property

132. UNRWA informed the Board that, in accordance with financial regulation 11.5, the following losses and write-offs had been recognized: cash losses of $2,165; inventory losses of $25,513, identified through inventory valuation; outstanding receivables of $941; property losses of $3.26 million; outstanding contribution receivables of $0.17 million and outstanding loans of $0.810 million (see annex II).

2. Ex gratia payments

133. As required by financial regulation 11.5, UNRWA reported ex gratia payments for 2015 amounting to $61,729, of which $59,322 (96 per cent) was paid to one staff member who lost her child at the Agency's Qalqilia Hospital owing to doctors' neglect. The remaining amount of $2,407 was paid to eight staff members for medical treatment for their children and to 14 staff who worked during a snow storm at the warehousing compound in the Syrian Arab Republic. A summary of the cases is contained in annex III to the present report.

3. Cases of fraud and presumptive fraud

134. In accordance with the International Standards on Auditing (ISA 240), the Board plans its audits of the financial statements so that it has a reasonable expectation of identifying material misstatements and irregularity, including those resulting from fraud. The Board's audit, however, should not be relied upon to identify all misstatements or irregularities. The primary responsibility for preventing and detecting fraud rests with management.

135. During the audit, the Board made enquiries of management regarding its responsibility for oversight in the assessment of risks of material fraud and the processes in place for identifying and responding to risks of fraud, including any specific risks that management has identified or which have been brought to its attention. The Board also enquired as to whether management had knowledge of any actual, suspected or alleged fraud, including enquiries to the Department of Internal Oversight Services. The additional terms of reference governing the external audit include cases of fraud and presumptive fraud in the list of matters that should be referred to in the Board's report.

136. In 2015 the Board did not identify any cases of fraud, other than those cases of fraud and presumptive fraud that have been reported by UNRWA and disclosed in the report. In accordance with article VII of the Financial Regulations and Rules of the United Nations and the related annex, UNRWA reported 41 cases of fraud and presumptive fraud to the Board during the period under review. Of the 41 cases, 19 investigations had been completed and finalized during the year, with quantified losses of $14,847. The other 22 cases are still under investigation and UNRWA will report on those cases next year. A summary of the cases is contained in annex IV to the present report.

D. Acknowledgement

137. The Board wishes to express its appreciation for the cooperation and assistance extended to its staff by the Commissioner-General and the members of his staff, as well as the staff at the Amman headquarters, the Gaza headquarters, the Jordan field office, the Gaza field office, the Lebanon field office and the field office in the Syrian Arab Republic.

(*Signed*) Mussa Juma **Assad**
Controller and Auditor-General of the United Republic of Tanzania
Chair of the United Nations Board of Auditors
(Lead Auditor)

(*Signed*) Sir Amyas C. E. **Morse**
Comptroller and Auditor-General of the
United Kingdom of Great Britain and Northern Ireland

(*Signed*) Shashi Kant **Sharma**
Comptroller and Auditor-General of India

Annex I

Status of implementation of recommendations for the period ended 31 December 2014

No.	Year of audit report	Paragraph reference	Board's recommendations	UNRWA response	Board's assessment	Implemented	Under implementation	Not implemented	Overtaken by events	Reiterated
1	2011 (A/67/5/ Add.3, chap. II)	82	The Board recommended that UNRWA allow for adequate tender submission time frames in accordance with the procurement manual; provide clarity on what constitutes "due cause"; and instruct field offices to institute adequate procurement planning.	The third version of the procurement manual (2015) addresses the concerns raised by the Board and the update has been completed. It is in the final stages of review. Upon submission of the revised manual to the Board, it is hoped that the recommendation can be closed. The procurement manual now has a timeline matrix for procurement notices and/or tender adverts. These are all the minimum number of working days required for the notices and/or adverts.	The Board considers the recommendation to have been implemented because the new enterprise resource planning system (known as REACH), which strengthens control processes over inventory lead time, together with the newly developed procurement manual that provides guidance on clear documentation of justifiable reasons for shortening tender periods, were found to be working.	X				
2	2011	118	The Board recommended that UNRWA enhance its supply manual to address the inconsistent procedures applied by its field offices in issuing inventories and that it address the gaps identified in the process of issuing inventories.	The Agency's enterprise resource planning system has just gone live. The business process related to issuing inventories is now coded into the system so there can be no other way to complete the tasks differently in the field offices. This addresses the Board's concern over a risk of inconsistencies under the previous paper system. The new system has done away with non-inventory and all goods are managed as inventory in the system now, creating the necessary consistency across the Agency.	The Board has verified that the new enterprise resource planning system has harmonized the supply procedures in all fields, therefore, the recommendation has been implemented.	X				

No.	Year of audit report	Paragraph reference	Board's recommendations	UNRWA response	Board's assessment	Implemented	Under implementation	Not implemented	Overtaken by events	Reiterated
3	2011	178	The Board recommended that UNRWA prioritize the implementation of internal audit recommendations, with emphasis on high risk areas identified by internal audit.	A standard operating procedure for audit recommendation follow-up has been drafted.	The Board acknowledges the measure taken by introducing a standard operating procedure, automating the follow-up process and implementing the 2011 and 2012 internal audit recommendations, and therefore closes this recommendation.	X				
4	2012 (A/68/5/ Add.3, chap. II)	62	The Board recommended that UNRWA develop a clear mechanism for monitoring supplier performance during the contract period. This would ensure compliance with regulations and would give management assurance that poor supplier performance was being addressed.	The technical instruction for the Contract Management Unit has been finalized, and In-Tend has been bought and is in use. Procurement and Logistics Division staff at headquarters have been trained on the use of In-Tend. It was to be officially launched in the first week of May 2016. Meanwhile, service contracts have been uploaded on In-Tend to enable a systematic tracking of suppliers' performance against set key performance indicators. Furthermore, according to the roll-out plan, In-Tend will be launched in the Jordan field office by the end of the third quarter of 2016, and in the remaining field offices by the end of the fourth quarter of 2016.	The implementation of the new enterprise resource planning system has been effected, however, system monitoring of service contracts is not yet effective. Meanwhile the Agency has procured In-Tend to enable a systematic tracking of suppliers' performance against set predefined key performance indicators, which is not yet fully operational. In addition, the technical instruction for the Contract Management Unit has not yet been approved by Human Resources.		X			

No.	Year of audit report	Paragraph reference	Board's recommendations	UNRWA response	Board's assessment	Implemented	Under implementation	Not implemented	Overtaken by events	Reiterated
5	2012	72	The Board recommended that UNRWA continue to mobilize resources to prevent buildings in bad condition from further deteriorating; prepare a comprehensive long-term asset management plan for its buildings in need of repair, as identified in the valuation report; and develop an asset repair and maintenance policy.	UNRWA has continued to mobilize resources and repair buildings as a priority for each field. The Agency will continue the implementation of repairs in accordance with the priority of categories of buildings requiring repair, as identified by the Agency's assessment. The asset management plan is to repair, monitor and assess on a regular basis. Assessment and implementation for routine maintenance purposes is continuing in all the field offices on a yearly basis. Implementation is carried out in accordance with an annual plan which is developed in each field, identifying priorities within available resources, on the basis of the yearly assessment. A maintenance policy and relevant technical instructions have already been issued.	The Board reviewed the progress and noted UNRWA efforts in mobilizing resources to ensure that maintenance is undertaken for at least a certain number of buildings each year. They have developed a long-term plan for construction, maintenance and rehabilitation of UNRWA premises in all field offices and it has been incorporated into the medium-term strategy (2016-2021). The Agency plans to prioritize fundraising in each year under its resource mobilization strategy.	X				
6	2012	82	The Board recommended that UNRWA endeavour to the best of its ability to obtain relevant documents to substantiate the right to use buildings and plots of land.	UNRWA is in the process of obtaining the relevant documentation.	Implementation of the recommendation is in progress; the Board reiterates its request that management liaise with governments of all the fields in which UNRWA operates to obtain the relevant documents.		X			

No.	Year of audit report	Paragraph reference	Board's recommendations	UNRWA response	Board's assessment	Implemented	Under implementation	Not implemented	Overtaken by events	Reiterated
7	2012	96	The Board recommended that UNRWA (a) formalize its results-based management results review processes in a policy or organizational directive; (b) ensure that the results review process takes place as envisaged, at midyear and on an annual basis; and (c) ensure that measures are implemented to support alternative means of collecting performance data from the Syrian Arab Republic field office, for example, though the Internet.	(a) Organizational directive No. 21 is still pending finalization, parts (b) and (c) have been implemented with a report from the Syrian Arab Republic field office submitted to the Board of Auditors.	The Board has assessed and is satisfied with part (b), but part (c) is subject to reviewing the report from the Syrian Arab Republic field office, while part (a) is subject to organizational directive No. 21 being approved.		X			
8	2012	101	The Board recommended that UNRWA: (a) set a time frame for establishing an information and communications technology steering committee to oversee the implementation and operation of information and communications technology-related functions; (b) develop a business case for deploying an electronic document management system that would act as a	(a) UNRWA established an information and communications technology steering committee, effective July 2013. Governance packages covering each aspect of the steering committee framework are in process. (b) Document retention, archive and disposal policy is currently being updated. Once completed, it will allow for the development of a detailed requirements document that will define future system requirements and allow UNRWA to more precisely specify the requirements to create an electronic document management system for	Organizational directive No. 26 covering the governance of information and communications technology, including the information and communications technology steering committee, has been developed and the Ramco team is no longer in existence as the new enterprise resource planning system replaced the previous one on 19 April 2015.				X	

No.	Year of audit report	Paragraph reference	Board's recommendations	UNRWA response	Board's assessment	Implemented	Under implementation	Not implemented	Overtaken by events	Reiterated
			key central repository accessible anywhere and at any time; and (c) set a time frame for and expedite the merging of the Ramco application support unit under the Finance Department with the application support unit under the Information Management Services Division.	digitization of paper records currently held at the central records unit. (c) The transition to a SAP platform requires an overall restructuring of the current information technology division and a merger with what will remain of the enterprise resource planning project team once that project closes at the end of 2015. By implication, the Ramco team will be disestablished in its entirety and be replaced by a support unit in the new information technology division.						
9	2012	112	The Board recommended that UNRWA continue monitoring the loan portfolio in the Syrian Arab Republic with a view to improving its operational self-sufficiency to a level that would enable it to cover its operational costs; improve controls by establishing a loan review committee for the management of loans receivable; and ensure that the general controls of the loan management information system are adequate for the mitigation of ever-growing business risks.	During 2013 the Agency's microfinance strategic outlook for the Microfinance Department in the Syrian Arab Republic was to minimize losses, to the extent possible, and to reach a level that would cover its operational costs, through developing strategies that meet the risk in the operations. Most importantly it was the currency risk. The Microfinance Department started to evaluate its loans receivable portfolio on a quarterly basis and to record the currency exchange losses. The Department was able to reallocate and manage currency devaluation in a better and more efficient way and was able to roll out the new information management system in early 2013, mitigating the operational	The Board reviewed and is satisfied with the remedial actions taken by the Microfinance Department to mitigate risks related to the Department's operations in the Syrian Arab Republic field office during 2013 and 2014, and is therefore closing the recommendation.	X				

No.	Year of audit report	Paragraph reference	Board's recommendations	UNRWA response	Board's assessment	Implemented	Under implementation	Not implemented	Overtaken by events	Reiterated
				risk. The system was tested in the audit of 2013, with a satisfactory outcome. A loan review committee was established to review loans receivable on a quarterly basis and advise management on compliance and any operational risks.						
10	2013 (A/69/5/Add.4, chap. II)	24	The Board reiterates its previous recommendation that UNRWA set up specific funding arrangements to fund its end-of-service liabilities, for consideration and approval by the appropriate authorities including the General Assembly.	UNRWA is focused on meeting the immediate humanitarian needs of Palestine refugees within a challenging operational environment. End-of-service liabilities would be addressed following a just and durable solution to the Palestine refugee question. Funding for an end-of-service liability, along with other potential obligations to staff and support to Palestine refugees delivered through UNRWA, would be developed in concert with appropriate authorities. Implementation of a comprehensive package of support will be contingent, once a just and durable solution has been reached, upon the financial support of the international community.	The end-of-service liabilities have not been funded and keep on increasing each year, the Board will therefore remain concerned over this situation until the Agency resolves how the liability will be funded. The recommendation was reiterated in 2014.					X
11	2013	31	The Board recommended that UNRWA identify specific IPSAS requirements that are more important in the preparation of financial statements and conduct training for staff in the Finance Department and other departments	As part of the launch of the new enterprise resource planning system, the Finance Department enhanced coordination with various departments relevant for the preparation of the financial statements and considered the applicable IPSAS in the implementation. Training was given to relevant staff across the field offices	The Board has verified that IPSAS training was conducted for the operational staff who are directly involved in the preparation of the final accounts and there has also been an improvement in the coordination with other departments, especially	X				

No.	Year of audit report	Paragraph reference	Board's recommendations	UNRWA response	Board's assessment	Implemented	Under implementation	Not implemented	Overtaken by events	Reiterated
			in order to enhance compliance; and improve coordination between the Finance Department and other departments during the preparation of financial statements to ensure reliability and completeness of reported balances.	regarding the new system and a detailed training manual was provided for reference.	the Procurement and Logistics Division. Hence, the recommendation is closed.					
12	2013	36	The Board recommended that UNRWA develop a policy on addressing fraud and other corrupt practices to guide management and other staff members in identifying and reporting fraud-related matters.	UNRWA accepts the recommendation and work is ongoing to produce an anti-corruption strategy to address the recommendation. The work is in response to a recommendation from the Advisory Committee on Internal Oversight to carry out a comprehensive assessment of the risks of fraud and corruption. Please note that the obligation of all staff members to report fraud, corruption and other forms of wrongdoing is laid out in general staff circular No. 5/2007. In addition, awareness on fraud, corruption and related reporting mechanisms is included in the Agency's ethics e-learning course that is mandatory for all staff, Agency-wide.	The Board has verified that UNRWA has issued an anti-fraud and anti-corruption policy and therefore considers that the recommendation has been implemented.	X				

No.	Year of audit report	Paragraph reference	Board's recommendations	UNRWA response	Board's assessment	Implemented	Under implementation	Not implemented	Overtaken by events	Reiterated
13	2013	40	The Board recommended that UNRWA undertake a mapping exercise to identify and document in a single document key internal controls for its critical business processes with reference to other documents providing detailed procedures.	UNRWA accepts the recommendation and will develop a document explaining roles and responsibilities for internal control relating to critical business processes.	Development of the document is still in progress.		X			
14	2013	43	The Board recommended that UNRWA: (a) develop and distribute to employees a risk management policy outlining the underlying approach to risk management and mitigating procedures; and (b) ensure that all high risks that are common to UNRWA are assessed and captured in the risk registers at the field offices, thus enabling the development of common procedures for responding to those risks.	UNRWA accepts the recommendation and will develop a document explaining roles and responsibilities for internal control relating to critical business processes. UNRWA has established a best practices for risk management and has a lot of evidence in this regard, including risk registers in the implementation plans for headquarters and the field for 2014-2015; risk registers and risk elements in the medium-term strategic plan for 2016-2021; risk elements in the document on priorities for 2015; risk assessments in quarterly reports to the Management Committee; risk analysis of projects in monthly assessments; and the Department of Internal Oversight Services developing its workplan on risk considerations. The Agency intends to develop and is committed to developing an organizational directive (No. 21) outlining the requirement for such practices.	The Board has reviewed the progress and is satisfied with the implementation of part (b) but part (a) is subject to development of organizational directive No. 21, which will outline the underlying practice.		X			

No.	Year of audit report	Paragraph reference	Board's recommendations	UNRWA response	Board's assessment	Implemented	Under implementation	Not implemented	Overtaken by events	Reiterated
				UNRWA has responded to the need for a greater focus on risk management in the Agency, including through the determination of acceptable levels of tolerance for certain risks. In line with a strengthened emphasis on risk management within the United Nations as a whole, the Agency has established and implemented a framework for risk management.						
15	2013	48	The Board recommended that UNRWA conduct a thorough review of the consultant's report and apply the proposed recommendations to improve the operations of the microcredit community support programme without compromising its basic mandate of helping Palestine refugees to achieve their full potential in human development.	Based on consultations with relief and support services at the field level (Jordan, Lebanon and the West Bank), field-specific recommendations were taken on board, including the freezing of the current lending mechanism in the Jordan field office and coming up with different lending tools, as well as the establishment of a loan tracking system and management information system in the Lebanon field office. However, on the specific recommendations made by the consultants to improve the performance of the microcredit community support programme, further action is being taken by fields to address those recommendations. UNRWA agrees with the recommendation, however it notes that in connection with the financial crisis, a decision has been made for 2016 to suspend funding for the microcredit community support programme until it can be	The implementation of the recommendation is in progress.		X			

No.	Year of audit report	Paragraph reference	Board's recommendations	UNRWA response	Board's assessment	Implemented	Under implementation	Not implemented	Overtaken by events	Reiterated
				aligned with the relief and support services reform criteria for addressing poverty.						
16	2013	53	The Board recommended that UNRWA: (a) expedite the implementation of a new software system for management of vehicles' workshop operations and record-keeping; and (b) enforce the available operational controls of the vehicles' workshop, including proper record-keeping and the completion of job card forms.	The fleet management system is in full use now in the West Bank and Jordan field offices, with both carlog and Fleetwave, which make up the fleet management system, in full use. Funding has been secured for the Lebanon field office, with 20 carlog packages bought for installation in 20 vehicles. Owing to the conflict in the Syrian Arab Republic, it has not yet been possible to install the system for that field office. The Gaza field office has carlog in use in all the vehicles. Fleetwave was to be introduced on 1 May 2016. The field offices are being continuously reminded about the requirement to use the maintenance module, which is an integral part of the Fleetwave system.	The system has been implemented in the West Bank and Jordan field offices, while the implementation for other field offices is still in progress. The Board insists that UNRWA expedite the full implementation of the recommendation.		X			
17	2013	58	The Board recommended that UNRWA expedite the evaluation process and adjust the opening and closing inventory balances accordingly to comply with IPSAS 12.	UNRWA is in the process of developing relevant policy and procedures relating to inventory and non-inventory goods in alignment with the enterprise resource planning system that was introduced during 2015. The procedures will be in accordance with IPSAS and take into account the recommendations of the Board.	Implemented subsequent to the introduction of the enterprise resource planning system, which considers the non-inventory items.	X				

No.	Year of audit report	Paragraph reference	Board's recommendations	UNRWA response	Board's assessment	Implemented	Under implementation	Not implemented	Overtaken by events	Reiterated
18	2013	63	The Board recommended that UNRWA include items procured under project funds during the preparation of procurement plans to benefit from economies of scale; and involve the Chief of the Procurement and Logistics Division and Field Procurement and Logistic Officers in the project-level procurement planning at headquarters and field levels to obtain input for the preparation of each procurement plan.	With the formal launch of the new procurement plans, all project procurement needs are now fully included in the procurement plans. The procurement plans cover both programme budget and project procurement planning, which allows the Procurement and Logistics Division to aggregate needs for bulk-buying and also attain economies of scale across the board. This also enables the strategic development of long-term agreements and collaboration within UNRWA, as well as with other United Nations entities. The Chief of Procurement and Logistics and field heads of procurement and logistics are all closely involved in the procurement planning process, also involving user departments and management. Many videoconferences, teleconferences and e-mail exchanges, as well as field visits, have taken place and will continue to do so in order to consolidate the procurement plans through a corporate-wide consultation and advice framework.	Implementation is in progress, as the Board review of the template for the Agency's corporate master procurement plan for 2016 noted the absence of the disclosure of the fund category which monitors all funds (i.e., programme budget, emergency appeals and projects). Therefore, the Board insists that the template be revised to accommodate details of funds.		X			
19	2013	66	The Board recommended that UNRWA: develop and implement a standard methodology and template for procurement planning to bring consistency	The third version of the procurement manual addresses the concerns raised by the Board. A standard methodology and procurement plan template has been developed and is in use at the corporate level. All the	The Board considers that the recommendation has been implemented, as UNRWA has issued the third version of the procurement manual and	X				

No.	Year of audit report	Paragraph reference	Board's recommendations	UNRWA response	Board's assessment	Implemented	Under implementation	Not implemented	Overtaken by events	Reiterated
			to its headquarters departments, field offices and project undertakings; and ensure procurement plans are thoroughly reviewed and agreed upon by the concerned departments, project managers and the Procurement and Logistics Division to ensure adequacy of their contents before implementation.	procurement needs for 2016 have been captured in the new procurement plans. Procurement plans are now reviewed and agreed upon by the concerned departments. The Procurement and Logistics Division ensures adequacy of their contents before implementation. Already there have been videoconferences, teleconferences and Skype calls, in which all the procurement plans received were fully discussed and contents confirmed for implementation. In addition to the calls, the Procurement and Logistics Division has held a face-to-face meeting with the Jordan field office wherein all the areas for collaboration were identified and are being worked on for implementation. The Division also visited the Lebanon field office to meet with field procurement and logistics officers from that office and the Syrian Arab Republic field office to discuss synergies and opportunities for collaboration. A similar visit is being planned for the West Bank and Gaza field offices. All the procurement plans have been fully reviewed and consolidated into a corporate master procurement Plan for strategic management and implementation.	established a template for the procurement plan. In addition, the procurement plans were found to have been reviewed.					

No.	Year of audit report	Paragraph reference	Board's recommendations	UNRWA response	Board's assessment	Implemented	Under implementation	Not implemented	Overtaken by events	Reiterated
20	2013	71	The Board recommended that UNRWA: enforce compliance with the procurement manual and minimize ex post facto approval and, where such approval is inevitable, clearly document the factors which necessitated the ex post facto approval; conduct detailed surveys and designs for construction work and ensure thorough review of survey reports to avoid unnecessary variations; and improve the process of reviewing the contents of each bill of quantities and ensure that all necessary items for a particular construction project are included before being approved.	The review documents, among other things, cover some awards made on an ex post facto basis, however this is not a major factor in UNRWA procurement practice. UNRWA does not agree with the notion that there is a systematic problem with unnecessary variations or agency estimates and/or bill of quantities. An independent review of designs and associated bills of quantities is a mandatory governance feature of the construction process and has been conducted as part of the process. The feature also reviews contract proposals asking for clearance of variation orders that exceed the tolerances defined in the procurement manual. Ex post facto: For any contract awarded pursuant to an emergency or operational urgency whose value is within the review threshold as set forth in appendix C, then the Director of Administrative Support (who may consult with the Advisory Committee on Procurement) or the Local Committee for Procurement, as applicable, shall perform the same review function as set out in section 2.4.3 of the procurement manual (2012), on an ex post facto basis. Where the value of the procurement action exceeds the review threshold of the	The Board reviewed the progress of the measures undertaken in field offices and was satisfied with those measures, including documentation of the reasons for ex post facto approval and the review process for the bill of quantities.	X				

No.	Year of audit report	Paragraph reference	Board's recommendations	UNRWA response	Board's assessment	Implemented	Under implementation	Not implemented	Overtaken by events	Reiterated
				relevant Procurement Committee set forth in appendix C to the procurement manual (2012), the awarding authority will ensure that the ex ante recommendation to waive competition or other requirements defined above has been obtained from the relevant Procurement Committee before the waiver is granted, or that the process to obtain the waiver is reviewed by the relevant Procurement Committee after the waiver was approved.						
21	2013	75	The Board recommended that UNRWA: (a) improve coordination between the Procurement and Logistics Division and users at the field offices to ensure that all procurement requirements are identified and communicated to the Procurement and Logistics Division at headquarters on a timely basis, to avoid the unnecessary shortening of the tender periods; (b) perform regular reviews of lead time and inventory balances to avoid emergency orders; and (c) review the grounds for waivers	The increased functionality provided by the procurement and supply management module of the newly implemented enterprise resource planning system demands that all projects are presented in a detailed way inside the system using the work breakdown structure. The structure will allow detailed identification of current and future procurement requirements and hence support planning efforts between headquarters and the field offices. The reporting functionality in SAP now includes enhanced inventory management and reporting tools that will also support demand planning. On the basis of the system having been introduced it is requested that parts (a) and (b) of the recommendation be	UNRWA has implemented the new enterprise resource planning system, which will enhance effective communication with the field on the inventory balance and lead time management. The Agency has also developed a third version of the procurement manual, which discusses waivers in detail. However, the Board noted similar weaknesses in the Gaza field office, indicating that the problem still exists. The Board will verify the effectiveness of the instituted		X			

No.	Year of audit report	Paragraph reference	Board's recommendations	UNRWA response	Board's assessment	Implemented	Under implementation	Not implemented	Overtaken by events	Reiterated
			to ensure they are consistent with current good practice.	closed. The third version of the procurement manual addresses the concerns mentioned in part (c), relating to waivers. Upon submission of the manual to the Board of Auditors, it is requested that the recommendation be closed. The enterprise resource planning system is now implemented and systemic improvements should be monitored over time in relation to this observation. Section 6.8.1 of the new procurement manual discusses waivers and other matters.	measures in the next audit.					
22	2013	81	The Board recommended that UNRWA: (a) establish a formal evaluation committee to enhance transparency, objectivity and equity in the bid evaluation process; (b) develop a standardized template for declarations of interest by evaluation committee members; and (c) design and document formal appointment letters for evaluation committee members.	(a) A standard operating procedure for the appointment of an independent formal bid evaluation committee is now in place, with bid evaluation committee members appointed through the formal process; (b) a standard template has also been established with a standard operating procedure for the declaration of conflicts of interest and assurance of confidentiality by all appointed bid evaluation committee members; (c) a corporate memorandum has been designed for the appointment of bid evaluation committee members.	The Agency introduced the third version of the procurement manual in October 2015. Therefore, the Board will verify the effectiveness of the measures employed during the next audit.		X			
23	2013	85	The Board recommended that UNRWA indicate the required financial resources for each strategic objective in	The medium-term strategy for 2016-2021 has been operationalized through the development of strategic plans for each field of UNRWA operation, which	In 2016, UNRWA does not consider implementation plans for headquarters and the field, but rather the annual operational		X			

No.	Year of audit report	Paragraph reference	Board's recommendations	UNRWA response	Board's assessment	Implemented	Under implementation	Not implemented	Overtaken by events	Reiterated
			the headquarters and field implementation plans for effective results evaluation.	cover the same strategic period of 2016-2021 and respond to the direction set in the medium-term strategy, detailing how the strategy will be tailored and implemented in each field. In addition to strategic plans, each of the five fields of UNRWA operation have developed an annual operational plan for 2016, designed to ensure alignment between the Agency's day-to-day work with the strategic priorities elaborated in the medium-term strategy. Together, strategic plans and annual operational plans replace biennial field implementation plans and the headquarters implementation plans used under the medium-term strategy for 2010-2015. Further to a request from the Board of Auditors, on 21 April 2016, an example of an annual operational plan budget (for the Jordan field office) was provided.	plan. The Board reviewed the annual operational plan and noted the operationalization of the medium-term strategy. However, despite the development of annual operational plans and instructions from the Department of Planning requiring the inclusion of financial resources for each strategic objective, the financial resources are still not included in the strategic objectives.					
24	2013	89	The Board recommended that UNRWA include the goal on internal governance and support in the upcoming medium-term strategy for 2016-2021 for consistency with implementation plans for headquarters and the field and the biennium budget.	The new medium-term strategy for 2016-2021 period will have a revised results framework that will include a management effectiveness component. Chapter 5 of the new strategy includes a goal on management and operational effectiveness, which is equivalent to the recommended goal on internal governance and support.	The recommendation is considered to have been implemented because the goal on internal governance and support has been included in the medium-term strategy of 2016-2021.	X				

No.	Year of audit report	Paragraph reference	Board's recommendations	UNRWA response	Board's assessment	Implemented	Under implementation	Not implemented	Overtaken by events	Reiterated
25	2013	93	The Board recommended that UNRWA: (a) establish a mechanism for mobilizing and uploading all vital project documents in the intranet on a regular basis; and (b) review the project process manual and specifically define the project officer responsible for maintaining and archiving all project documents in one location.	(a) Implemented: documents that relate to project management are uploaded on the intranet (Department of Planning page). Documents that are specific to grant agreements are uploaded into a Department of External Relations and Communications database accessible to concerned staff; and (b) the project procedures manual has been updated to reflect, among other things, the environment subsequent to the introduction of the enterprise resource planning system. The finalization of the project procedures manual has been delayed by the priorities relating to the launch of the system.	The Board's assessment is that part (a) has been implemented; part (b) is subject to review of the project procedures manual.		X			
26	2013	97	The Board recommended that UNRWA: (a) monitor the current trend with regard to programme support costs and ensure that the amount charged is in line with the approved standard rate; and (b) ensure that any deviation from the standard rate is agreed upon by donors and approved by the Director of Finance on the basis of a valid and documented justification.	Any exceptional deviations from standard programme support cost rates as per the technical instruction No. 22, such as those requested by specific donors to the Nahr el-Bared camp project, are subject to approval by the Director of Finance based on written justification provided by the Department of External Relations and Communications.	The Board reviewed the programme support cost recovery rates charged to the projects income under Nahr el-Bared camp and noted that they are now in line with technical instruction No. 22 and those that were against the technical instruction were approved by the Director of Finance. In addition, UNRWA has streamlined the approval process of programme support cost rate through the new enterprise resource planning system, which has a	X				

No.	Year of audit report	Paragraph reference	Board's recommendations	UNRWA response	Board's assessment	Implemented	Under implementation	Not implemented	Overtaken by events	Reiterated
					specific module dealing with project management. They have configured the standard rate to be charged.					
27	2013	102	The Board recommended that UNRWA: (a) expedite recruitment of the specific project manager for Nahr el-Bared Refugee Camp; and (b) ensure the timely submission of designs and all project requirements to the Directorate General for Urban Planning in Lebanon for clearance to avoid further delays and future cost overruns.	(a) The Project Manager for Nahr el-Bared Refugee Camp has been recruited; (b) to ensure the timely submission of design and all related project requirements to the Directorate General for Urban Planning for clearance to avoid further delays and future cost overruns, communications with the Directorate for clearance and preliminary meetings with the consultant acting on behalf of the Government of Lebanon in relation to the matter have already taken place. The submission of documentation to the Directorate follows the completion of a validation and preliminary design process, in line with the established participatory design process. The designs and all project requirements were submitted to the Directorate General for Urban Planning in Lebanon for clearance, in June 2015.	The Board assessed that part (a) has been implemented and that for part (b) the designs and all project requirements were submitted to the Directorate General for Urban Planning in Lebanon for clearance in June 2015.	X				
28	2013	108	The Board recommended that UNRWA: (a) establish steering committees for construction projects as currently required in the project process manual, while waiting for the	The update to the project procedures manual is linked to the implementation of the new enterprise resource planning system, which was introduced in April 2015. The project procedures manual is already being updated but will not be completed before the	The Board assessed that finalization of the implementation of the recommendation is subject to updating of the project procedures manual.		X			

No.	Year of audit report	Paragraph reference	Board's recommendations	UNRWA response	Board's assessment	Implemented	Under implementation	Not implemented	Overtaken by events	Reiterated
			revised manual; and (b) review the project process manual and provide clear guidance on the establishment of project steering committees, including with regard to the composition of the committees and on the roles and responsibilities of their members, and guidance on the kinds of projects that require a steering committee.	implementation of the enterprise resource planning (so as to ensure the manual provides clear and correct guidance). The processes and tools for the manual, such as a steering committee, are included in the update to the manual. The finalization of the manual has been delayed owing to priorities relating to the launch of the enterprise resource planning system.						
29	2013	112	The Board recommended that UNRWA: (a) ensure that evidence of staff attendance in an induction course is filed in their respective personal files; (b) consider allocating funds to cover the cost of induction courses in the forthcoming biennium budget; and (c) consider alternative methods, other than classroom training (such as e-learning), for delivering induction courses at a lower cost where there are budget constraints.	The last induction course took place on 25 June 2014 and attendance records are placed in staff members' files. Future orientation courses are planned for 2015/2016. Meanwhile, as an alternative method, in June 2014, human resources at the Lebanon field office put together a comprehensive orientation booklet that is sent to all new staff members as an integral part of the appointment package. Signed confirmation letters (indicating the receipt of the orientation handbook) are placed in each new staff member's file as of that date.	The Board has reviewed the evidence and is satisfied with the implementation.	X				

No.	Year of audit report	Paragraph reference	Board's recommendations	UNRWA response	Board's assessment	Implemented	Under implementation	Not implemented	Overtaken by events	Reiterated
30	2013	117	The Board recommended that UNRWA incorporate the identification of individual staff training needs in its performance evaluation process, to minimize costs.	The new ePer system has been implemented in all five fields of operation for international and senior area staff. All other staff have been included in the system as of the fourth quarter of 2015. Meanwhile, individual staff learning needs have been included in the existing system. UNRWA therefore considers the recommendation closed and will seek concurrence from the Board of Auditors for its closure.	The Board reviewed the ePer system, which includes the needs assessment in its online performance appraisal, and therefore considers that the recommendation has been implemented.	X				
31	2013	121	The Board recommended that UNRWA review the staff table by performing detailed assessments so as to eliminate redundant posts and identify key posts that need to be filled in a timely manner in order to enhance the delivery of services to refugees.	The staffing resources are regularly reviewed. An international staffing review was conducted in November 2012 to ensure that the Agency's scarce international staffing resources are allocated in an optimal way. The review recommended three posts to be considered for redeployment. This was not confirmed and therefore, the posts remain allocated as they were. The annual class formation exercise regularly reviews the allocation of education staff (two thirds of the Agency's staff members fall under this category) and is one of the main workforce planning exercises, as it concerns the majority of staff members. It is a continuous process and the final report is not yet available.	The Board has reviewed the draft results of the staffing review, including the staff table for area staff, and raised some comments for clarification from the Department of Human Resources, which have not been addressed.		X			

No.	Year of audit report	Paragraph reference	Board's recommendations	UNRWA response	Board's assessment	Implemented	Under implementation	Not implemented	Overtaken by events	Reiterated
32	2013	126	The Board recommended that UNRWA expedite the planned initiatives to reduce the length of the recruitment process and to enhance the timely delivery of services to refugees.	The recommendations are based on observations in the Lebanon field office, which indicated that the following initiatives are planned: (a) preparation of an annual recruitment plan; (b) weekly updates to departments; and (c) regular meetings with departments; the annual recruitment plan is currently prepared and the weekly updates and regular meetings are already ongoing.	The recommendation was reiterated in 2014 as the issue still exists in Lebanon and Jordan field offices and the headquarters in Amman, according to the Board's assessment during the year. In 2015, the Board noted that among the 26 recruitments of area staff that took place, the recruitment process in 20 cases exceeded 90 days and the average period was 129 days, while for international posts, out of 40 recruitment processes in 2015, 14 exceeded 120 days, although the average period was 106 days.					X
33	2013	130	The Board recommended that UNRWA actively follow up with the Executive Office of the Secretary-General and the power service provider, to find a lasting solution on the settlement of the electricity bills, to avoid the risk of power disconnection in refugees camps.	The Lebanon field office and the Commissioner-General have actively followed up with the power service provider and the Government of Lebanon to explain that UNRWA is not responsible for settling any individual debts of Palestine refugees, including settling fees for power consumption, whether inside or outside the camps. However, this has not led to a resolution. With respect to the recommendation that UNRWA actively follow up with the Executive Office of the Secretary-General, UNRWA	The Board acknowledges management initiatives and follow-up with regard to the issue, however, the recommendation cannot be closed as the matter is still in progress and the unsettled electricity bills continue to appear in UNRWA financial statements as a contingent liability.		X			

No.	Year of audit report	Paragraph reference	Board's recommendations	UNRWA response	Board's assessment	Implemented	Under implementation	Not implemented	Overtaken by events	Reiterated
				advises that the Executive Office and the Office of Legal Affairs had decided with UNRWA that the Agency's representative office in New York would present the démarche to the Permanent Mission of Lebanon to the United Nations. UNRWA did so in 2012, but a resolution was not reached. The Permanent Mission subsequently indicated to the Assistant Secretary-General for Legal Affairs, in 2014, that it wanted to discuss the matter at a technical level with UNRWA. When the Lebanon field office followed up with the Government of Lebanon, the Government took the position that the issue is between UNRWA and the power service provider only.						
34	2013	134	The Board recommended that UNRWA develop a contingency plan to support the existing enterprise resource planning system in case of further delays in the implementation of the new system.	The new enterprise resource planning system was introduced on 19 April 2015 and the contract with Ramco has been extended, for future reference and audit purposes, until 2019.	The Board considers the recommendation to be implemented because UNRWA has extended the contract with Ramco.	X				
35	2013	155	The Board recommended that UNRWA develop a benefits realization plan for the enterprise resource planning project and integrate it with the project master plan to ensure	A new version of the project plan has been created, that includes the requested details. That version is periodically updated. A benefits realization plan (subsequently revised to be known as the business case) with quantitative measures is currently being	The recommendation has been reiterated in 2015 as the issue still exists.					X

No.	Year of audit report	Paragraph reference	Board's recommendations	UNRWA response	Board's assessment	Implemented	Under implementation	Not implemented	Overtaken by events	Reiterated
			effective monitoring and the realization of benefits.	finalized, to be completed September 2015.						
36	2013	164	The Board recommended that UNRWA: (a) develop appropriate procedures for erasing information contained in information and communications technology, taking into consideration the sensitivity of the information being handed over to the disposal authorities; and (b) develop security guidelines based on good practices for protecting critical information on mobile devices.	The recruitment process is ongoing for an information and security officer who will handle all security matters. Upon onboarding, the recommendation will be included in the incumbent's workplan for completion by the end of 2016. In the meantime, the Information Management Services Division has started a campaign, with guidelines rolled out Agency-wide to raise awareness of data integrity, confidentiality and availability, containing practical good practice tips that users can easily follow.	The implementation is still in progress.		X			
37	2013	170	The Board recommended that UNRWA: (a) through its field and department directors, ensure that investigation cases are recorded in the case management system accurately and on a timely basis; and (b) recruit additional professional investigators who would report direct to the Investigations Division of the Department of Internal Oversight Services	UNRWA will put in place a mechanism to ensure that the case management system is completed on a timely basis and that the data are complete and accurate. With respect to additional professional investigators, the Department of Internal Oversight Services initiated and completed the recruitment of two P-3 professional investigators in 2014 to strengthen the support it can provide to field-led investigations. In accordance with the Department's organizational directive those staff members (investigators) will provide technical advice,	Implementation of the recommendation is in progress: in 2014 the Agency succeeded in recruiting two P-3 professional investigators at two field offices, while the other three field offices lack professional investigators. The Board reviewed the system and was satisfied with the process of recording cases and timely updates on cases from the field.		X			

No.	Year of audit report	Paragraph reference	Board's recommendations	UNRWA response	Board's assessment	Implemented	Under implementation	Not implemented	Overtaken by events	Reiterated
			and supervise staff involved in investigations at the field offices.	guidance and training to field staff that carry out such investigations, supervised by field directors. The extent to which the staff investigators would be directly involved in supervising the field staff carrying out investigations is a matter that would depend on the nature of the case, and would be discussed and agreed between the Department and the field directors, as and when the need arises. The need for additional investigators will be assessed on a regular basis through the Department's annual workplan.						
38	2013	174	The Board recommended that UNRWA (a) expedite the finalization of the evaluation framework to guide and support the evaluation functions within the Agency; and (b) review the current practice of handling evaluation activities at headquarters departments and field offices on an ad hoc basis, with a view to improving the evaluation function.	(a) The framework guiding and supporting the centralized and decentralized evaluation function has been drafted, including a quality assurance framework and an evaluation policy. The quality assurance framework was discussed with technical staff engaged in evaluation in UNRWA, with senior management and with the Advisory Committee on Internal Oversight, and presented to the peer review of the evaluation function. The evaluation policy was discussed with senior management, the Advisory Committee on Internal Oversight and with the peer review panel. Comments will be integrated and the policy tabled at a management committee meeting for final endorsement; (b) the quality	The recommendation is still in progress as the documents are not yet approved.		X			

No.	Year of audit report	Paragraph reference	Board's recommendations	UNRWA response	Board's assessment	Implemented	Under implementation	Not implemented	Overtaken by events	Reiterated
				assurance framework and the policy include elements to ensure more systematic planning for evaluations.						
39	2013	180	The Board recommended that UNRWA enhance the internal control system by expediting the implementation of high-risk internal audit recommendations.	As part of its semi-annual audit recommendation follow-up process, the Department of Internal Oversight Services will continue to focus management's attention on addressing the open high-risk recommendations.	The Board noted that of the 44 recommendations outstanding as of 2013, 9 per cent were not implemented and 11 per cent were under implementation. The Board has reiterated the recommendation in the present report.					X
40	2013	185	The Board recommended that the Microfinance Department: (a) improve controls by establishing an online loan application in the new Omni enterprise system in 2014; and (b) closely supervise cashiers' activities and issue instructions to the operations team to strictly follow the operational procedures and adopt proper follow-up procedures to address late payments.	Part (a) has already been completed and is now part of the loan application procedure. Part (b) was also completed and the procedural manual updated. Staff were trained on the correct procedures and increased supervision of the branches introduced to ensure compliance.	The recommendation is still outstanding, the latest review done by the Board of the Deloitte working papers noted that the weaknesses still exist. The Board has reiterated the recommendation.					X
41	2013	188	The Board recommended that the Microfinance Department pass proper adjusting entries in 2014 to match balances from the register to the	This was being done on a quarterly basis in 2014 from the Financial Management System. With the introduction of the new system, the Microfinance Department will have direct access to the asset module and this will no	A new fixed assets module was created in the new system that is linked and reconciled with the fixed assets register. The Board reviewed the internal audit	X				

No.	Year of audit report	Paragraph reference	Board's recommendations	UNRWA response	Board's assessment	Implemented	Under implementation	Not implemented	Overtaken by events	Reiterated
			ledger by category and include fixed asset modules in the new enterprise resource planning system, which would maintain the link between the asset register and the ledger.	longer require adjusting entries, but the system will only be operating in 2015.	work with regard to the Microfinance Department's new fixed assets register and noted a reclassification journal with entries made during the year to adjust opening balances to reconcile ledger balances with new fixed assets register.					
42	2013	192	The Board recommended that the Microfinance Department develop a formal policy and procedure for transferring files exported from the Omni system to the Ramco system and that it establish a uniform naming convention for all UNRWA information technology resources, including the network and the Omni application.	This is currently done through an interface file that is uploaded to Ramco each month and then all loan accounts are reconciled between both systems. This will be further enhanced once the new system is operational.	The Board reviewed the Microfinance Department's internal auditors working paper and confirmed the existence of an interface between Omni and the new enterprise resource planning system.	X				
43	2014 (A/70/5/ Add.4, chap. II)	23	The Board recommended that UNRWA: (a) liaise with United Nations Headquarters to obtain confirmation on the approach to be followed to settle its end-of-service liabilities; and (b) avoid decisions that increase these	This is the only recommendation with which UNRWA disagrees, since it is considered to be impractical given its mandated responsibilities. The matter of the unfunded severance liability (amounting to $525 million as at 31 December 2014) is inherently tied to the nature of the Agency and its temporary	The Board has assessed the end-of-service liability and noted an increase of 24 per cent owing to an increase in the computation formula from 11 per cent to 12 per cent of the completed years of service, with effect from January 2015,			X		

No.	Year of audit report	Paragraph reference	Board's recommendations	UNRWA response	Board's assessment	Implemented	Under implementation	Not implemented	Overtaken by events	Reiterated
			liabilities while its funding is still uncertain.	mandate. It is fully expected that when there is a sustainable political solution resolving the displacement of Palestine refugees, that solution will address, among other matters, the future of UNRWA activities, along with the dissolution of its assets and liabilities. In addition, the Agency has already initiated a series of austerity measures, including voluntary early retirement schemes and reductions in class size as part of the effort to reduce staff costs, all of which contribute to not increasing the end-of-service liabilities while funding is still uncertain.	and a decrease in the discount rate from 4.75 to 4.32.					
44	2014	27	The Board recommended that UNRWA: (a) establish a rigorous review process of its financial information during the preparation of financial statements at field offices in order to reduce the recurring non-compliance with accounting policies and procedures evident in some fields; (b) ensure that officers involved in the preparation of financial statements at the field offices have adequate support from Headquarters with regard to the practical	With the introduction of the new enterprise resource planning system, policies and procedures in all the field offices are now consistent through controls embedded in the system. Furthermore, as part of the implementation and subsequent to the launch, there has been extensive coordination between the Department of Finance at headquarters and field offices to ensure accuracy of data migration and unified application. The IPSAS section at the Department of Finance is available at all times to support the field offices on any queries they may have on IPSAS application. All vendors are now part of the accounts	The Board reviewed the financial statements and noted recurrent weaknesses such as the non-performance of reconciliation of vendors' balances at year-end to identify unrecorded payables or payments, as required by the finance technical instruction of 2013. The Board noted two vendors for which reconciliation has not been done since 2002. In this regard the recommendation has been reiterated.					X

No.	Year of audit report	Paragraph reference	Board's recommendations	UNRWA response	Board's assessment	Implemented	Under implementation	Not implemented	Overtaken by events	Reiterated
			application of IPSAS requirements; and (c) ensure that the reconciliation of vendors' balances at year-end is done in order to identify unrecorded payables or payments.	payable module in the new system and it is anticipated that the reconciliation of vendors' balances at year-end will be performed in a timely manner to mitigate the risk of unrecorded payables/payments. Weekly meetings are held between headquarters and the field on implementation issues relating to the new system, including IPSAS application and year-end reconciliation of vendors' balances.						
45	2014	31	The Board recommended that UNRWA: (a) review its follow-up strategy to improve and strengthen its efforts to collect the long outstanding VAT arrears; and (b) review the collectability of the receivables and impair the value for amounts considered as uncollectable.	The matter is being spearheaded by the Department of Legal Affairs and UNRWA entered into arrangements in 2013 with regard to exemption from VAT for purchases in the West Bank and Gaza. In August 2015, the advance VAT exemption arrangement for Gaza was fully implemented. The Agency continues to raise the issue, notably through the annual report submitted to the General Assembly by the Commissioner-General, which is considered by the Special Political and Decolonization Committee. The matter is also under the active consideration of the Working Group on the Financing of UNRWA.	The Board reviewed the progress and discussed the same with the Director of Finance and noted that discussion is ongoing with the Palestinian Authority on the payment of VAT receivables. The Palestinian Authority is planning to offset arrears of VAT receivables against services bills such as electricity bills.		X			

No.	Year of audit report	Paragraph reference	Board's recommendations	UNRWA response	Board's assessment	Implemented	Under implementation	Not implemented	Overtaken by events	Reiterated
46	2014	35	The Board recommended that UNRWA develop a mechanism for tracking and quantifying the net savings from austerity measures at all levels of operation and evaluate their effectiveness.	Savings from austerity measures are tracked by UNRWA centrally under the specific guidance of the Deputy Commissioner-General with assistance from all departments including Finance, Human Resources and the Executive Office.	The Board reviewed the instruction on austerity measures from the Deputy Commissioner-General; however, there is no evidence as to how the tracking across all departments is done.		X			
47	2014	39	The Board recommended that UNRWA: (a) develop an Agency-wide management information system to harmonize information on the microcredit community support programme for the purpose of decision-making and to enable impact assessment, as well as the aggregation of data in the general financial statements; and (b) expedite finalization of the memorandum of understanding to make it legally binding.	In the light of the financial situation, a decision was made for 2016 to suspend funding for the microcredit community support programme until it can be aligned with the relief and support services reform criteria for addressing poverty. 2015 and 2016 plans include the continued work of the Jordan field office to prepare the by-laws for guiding community-based organizations engagement with UNRWA as a prerequisite for funding. Further, a budget decision for 2016 was taken in support of a freeze on direct grants for such organizations and only activity-based support for programmes relating to persons with disabilities and women will be granted.	The Board has reviewed the progress of implementation and considered the recommendation to be under implementation.		X			

No.	Year of audit report	Paragraph reference	Board's recommendations	UNRWA response	Board's assessment	Implemented	Under implementation	Not implemented	Overtaken by events	Reiterated
48	2014	42	The Board recommended that UNRWA formally define and document the criteria for issuing additional loans.	A decision was made for 2016 to suspend funding for the microcredit community support programme until it can be aligned with the relief and support services reform criteria for addressing poverty. The recommendation can be considered to have been overtaken by events.	The Board assessed the progress and noted that initially, the Jordan field office stated that it was developing the criteria for issuing additional loans; however, it has suspended that work pending further guidance from headquarters in Amman on the reform. In this regard, it considered the recommendation to be under implementation.		X			
49	2014	45	The Board recommended that UNRWA: (a) expedite the process of developing its maintenance policy to guide building maintenance work; and (b) develop a database system for maintenance records to provide reliable information for decision-making.	The recommendations were accepted by the department of Infrastructure and Camp Improvement and were implemented, with completion in the fourth quarter of 2015. The results of that implementation were submitted to the Board of Auditors as part of the annual audit in the first quarter of 2016.	The Board has reviewed the maintenance policy and inspected the database, therefore it considers the recommendation to have been implemented.	X				
50	2014	49	The Board recommended that UNRWA ensure all procurement waivers and deviations from the provisions of the UNRWA procurement manual (2012) are requested and approved by the director of the	The Procurement and Logistics Division obtained a signed waiver from the Director of the Jordan field office for every request pertaining to the shortening of the tender period, and for every request by the user to retender, as well as for any procurement actions that deviated from the requirements of the	Since January 2015, UNRWA has established two separate waiver files that are kept at the front office and the Procurement and Logistics Division, comprising all waivers requested and approved during the	X				

No.	Year of audit report	Paragraph reference	Board's recommendations	UNRWA response	Board's assessment	Implemented	Under implementation	Not implemented	Overtaken by events	Reiterated
			respective field office or by the Chief of the Procurement and Logistics Division.	procurement manual. The Division keeps updated records of all waivers obtained within the Division's delegation of authority.	year. Therefore the recommendation is considered to have been implemented.					
51	2014	55	The Board recommended that UNRWA: (a) establish mechanisms to allow regular review of engineers' estimates prior to tendering, which will help the Agency to arrive at cost estimates based on the prevailing market price; (b) review the retendering trend and establish ways of minimizing it; and (c) facilitate site visits by interested bidders to enable proper evaluation of the scope of work and cost estimates.	Part (a) is in progress, the Procurement and Logistics Division, the Engineering and Construction Services Department and the Infrastructure and Camp Improvement Programme will review standard operating procedures for contracts by the end of September 2015, which includes the following considerations: (i) an increase in the frequency of updating the Agency estimates, possibly on a quarterly basis so as to be more consistent with the market prices; and (ii) considering establishing a review committee to validate the field estimates prior to each tender; part (b) as for negotiations with the lowest bidder, in principle, negotiations are usually not undertaken subsequent to a competitive selection process. However, negotiations may still be necessary after a competitive tender in order to ensure best value for money for UNRWA. For more information regarding negotiation conditions, please refer to para. 8.4.7 (page 76 of the procurement manual); part (c) as detailed above in part (a), the quarterly review of the Agency estimates will guarantee up-to-date pricing	The Board has reviewed the instituted measures; however, their effectiveness will be assessed during the next audit.		X			

No.	Year of audit report	Paragraph reference	Board's recommendations	UNRWA response	Board's assessment	Implemented	Under implementation	Not implemented	Overtaken by events	Reiterated
				in order for each tender to reflect most accurately the market prices for construction materials.						
52	2014	56	The Board recommended that UNRWA: (a) ensure that all service contracts are signed before service delivery to make them legally binding; and (b) conduct performance evaluations of previous services rendered before extending service contracts.	During the visit of the Board, no hospital performance evaluation was performed for the previous two years, as reported. The most recent evaluation was performed in 2011/2012, samples of which were submitted to the Board of Auditors. Such a task is mandatory as a supplementary prerequisite for the validation of any hospital contract completion or further extension. Accordingly, hospital performance evaluation shall be performed on a yearly basis in line with contract issuance, and the evaluation for 2015 is in progress. In addition, for 2016, and in coordination with the Procurement and Logistics Division, UNRWA will ensure that service contracts are issued before services delivery.	The Board has noted the management response; however, the verification of progress will be done during the next audit.		X			
53	2014	60	The Board recommended that UNRWA: (a) expedite the review of its standard operating procedures to facilitate the generation of the consolidated procurement plan and ensure that plans are approved by existing procurement	Part (a) the third version of the procurement plan, which also has guidelines and standard operating procedures for procurement planning and a framework for the generation of a consolidated procurement plan, was launched in October 2015. The creation and submission of procurement plans for headquarters and the field offices is now a mandatory	The Board has not received an actual consolidated procurement plan, though UNRWA managed to establish a template and guidelines and standard operating procedures for procurement planning and a framework for the generation of a		X			

No.	Year of audit report	Paragraph reference	Board's recommendations	UNRWA response	Board's assessment	Implemented	Under implementation	Not implemented	Overtaken by events	Reiterated
			committees before implementation; and (b) improve the preparation of procurement plans at the field offices to include key elements for evaluation and accountability.	requirement in the new procurement manual; part (b) the approval of procurement plans is also a requirement as stipulated in the procurement plan and the ensued corporate inter-office memorandum issued by the Chief of the Procurement and Logistics Division to all directors and heads of procurement and logistics at headquarters and field offices; and part (c) the new procurement manual's mandatory requirement for procurement plans, the provision of a corporate procurement plan template, the support provided by the Procurement and Logistics Division to field offices through videoconferences, teleconferences and e-mails have improved the preparation of procurement plans at headquarters and field offices, with the framework for ongoing evaluation and accountability having been established.	consolidated procurement plan, therefore the recommendation is categorized as under implementation.					
54	2014	63	The Board recommended that UNRWA: (a) establish a dedicated contracts management desk office within UNRWA that will act as coordinator for the Agency's contractual relationships; (b) create an effective relationship between the management and	Part (a) a dedicated Contracts Management Unit has now been established in the Procurement and Logistics Division, with the Head of the Unit serving as the main focal point for all contract management issues. The Unit is up and running with dedicated staff. The Unit still needs formal recognition from Human Resources and the formal adoption of the new	The recommendation is in progress, as the structure is not yet approved. In addition, the issue of liquidated damages will be reviewed in all field offices during the next audit, in 2016.		X			

No.	Year of audit report	Paragraph reference	Board's recommendations	UNRWA response	Board's assessment	Implemented	Under implementation	Not implemented	Overtaken by events	Reiterated
			suppliers and maintain regular communication with suppliers; and (c) consider the inclusion of a liquidated damages clause in the contracts relating to medicines and medical supplies to enforce the compliance of suppliers.	terms of reference and grades of staff therein, also by Human Resources; part (b) an effective supplier relationship management platform has been established with the Contracts Management Unit as the lead focal point for UNRWA. The Unit is involved in all stages of the process for awarding contracts and the issuance of purchase orders. The suppliers are also informed by the Unit when buyers dispatch purchase orders; part (c) the liquidated damages clause is now included for the procurement of all goods, services and works, including medicines and medical supplies, and compliance is monitored by the Contract Management Unit. In addition, a corporate memo was sent to staff of the Procurement and Logistics Division to ensure that the procedures are maintained in practice across the board. A sample purchase order with the instruction to suppliers to sign a copy and return to UNRWA as an acknowledgement and acceptance, as well as UNRWA general and special conditions are attached to all purchase orders dispatched to suppliers, including the liquidated damages clause. Performance bonds are also taken.						

No.	Year of audit report	Paragraph reference	Board's recommendations	UNRWA response	Board's assessment	Implemented	Under implementation	Not implemented	Overtaken by events	Reiterated
55	2014	67	The Board recommended that UNRWA: (a) expedite the construction of one school, namely the fully green school, for the consolidation of three schools presently being operated in rented buildings; (b) consider developing long-term plans for the replacement of schools operated in rented buildings and short-term solutions for equipping the rented schools; and (c) given the limited resources of the Agency, continue efforts to mobilize funds to meet the costs of land and construction.	As the Board has already noted, the Agency is currently experiencing financial difficulties, with limited resources. It was unlikely that UNRWA would be able to address the recommendation in 2015 and the Agency will continue to mobilize its limited funds, focusing on core activities and priorities.	The Board reviewed the progress on the mobilization of resources for construction of the school; however, its progress is suspended owing to financial difficulties.		X			
56	2014	68	The Board recommended that UNRWA: (a) allocate learning resource rooms in existing schools to enhance implementation of special educational needs programmes; and (b) mobilize sufficient resources to renovate existing school buildings to allow easy access for students with mobility problems.	As the Board has already noted, the Agency is currently experiencing financial difficulties, with limited resources. It is unlikely that UNRWA will be able to address the recommendation in 2015 and the Agency will continue to mobilize its limited funds, focusing on core activities and priorities.	The Board has reviewed the progress, including the plan for implementation; however, it is suspended owing to financial difficulties.		X			

No.	Year of audit report	Paragraph reference	Board's recommendations	UNRWA response	Board's assessment	Implemented	Under implementation	Not implemented	Overtaken by events	Reiterated
57	2014	70	The Board recommended that UNRWA: (a) ensure that field offices expedite the recruitment process for the vacant posts within the new structure and coordinate with the Department of Education at UNRWA headquarters on matters requiring headquarters decisions; and (b) expedite the finalization of the draft governance framework to support the implementation of the education reform strategy.	Part (a) the recruitment for the vacant posts in the new structure was accelerated and has been completed in 4 of the 5 fields. Final steps are contingent on the funding situation; part (b) the drafting of the governance framework is ongoing.	The Board reviewed the status and considered the recommendation to be under implementation.		X			
58	2014	71	The Board recommended that UNRWA: establish acceptable strategies to avoid Agency-wide effects resulting from the actions of the area staff union on the implementation of the teacher coordinators pilot project at other field offices.	Following field difficulties for the pilot project in the West Bank, it was transferred to Lebanon in 2014. Owing to the financial difficulties of the organization, the pilot project has also been held up in Lebanon, but the Agency is pursuing its continuation.	The Board reviewed the status and considered the recommendation to be under implementation.		X			
59	2014	76	The Board recommended that UNRWA: (a) explore the possibility of entering into long-term agreements with local suppliers that	The audit recommendation is closed: the Procurement and Logistics Division and Health Department met with the Chief of the Division in July 2015 and agreed that the Procurement and Logistics	The Board visited the cold rooms and conducted interviews with responsible staff. The cold rooms are working and identified other areas		X			

No.	Year of audit report	Paragraph reference	Board's recommendations	UNRWA response	Board's assessment	Implemented	Under implementation	Not implemented	Overtaken by events	Reiterated
			offer competitive prices and meet the required specifications; (b) expedite the installation of new cold rooms to provide enough space for drugs that need to be stored at temperatures below 8°C; and (c) dispose of the expired drugs to create additional storage space and, in the intervening period, allocate temporary storage space to provide adequate drug storage facilities.	Division would resolve the problem of late delivery and pricing through a combination of activities: enhanced and improved contract management; broadening the supplier base both locally and internationally by introducing generic pharmaceutical supplies also approved by the Jordan Food and Drug Administration; and conducting a yearly quantification exercise to allow for more precise estimation of requirements.	within the building allocated for the Procurement and Logistics Division. Therefore, parts (b) and (c) are implemented while part (a) is in progress as there is no supporting document to substantiate the Agency's response.					
60	2014	80	The Board recommended that UNRWA develop and implement procedures to facilitate quality control tests of essential medicines and medical supplies at the Lebanon field office.	The pharmaceutical testing of medical supplies is not performed upon receipt of such goods, rather it is done by the manufacturer in the country of origin. The only requirement of the Ministry of Public Health is to ensure the medicines are registered in Lebanon and cleared by the Ministry. In other words, all medical supplies entering Lebanon shall obtain approvals to enter the country according to Ministry of Public Health regulations. Pharmaceutical inspection is being performed prior to the release of shipments of medical supplies at the port of discharge.	The Board reviewed the plan for developing procedures to facilitate quality control tests at the Lebanon field office; however, its implementation is limited by financial difficulties.		X			

No.	Year of audit report	Paragraph reference	Board's recommendations	UNRWA response	Board's assessment	Implemented	Under implementation	Not implemented	Overtaken by events	Reiterated
61	2014	81	The Board recommended that UNRWA identify appropriate means and areas for waste disposal and consider the inclusion of waste management in the annual budget as a priority in order to facilitate the establishment of disposal facilities at the health centres.	A waste management plan has been developed and approved by the front office. The Department of Health will coordinate internally to secure the required funds in order to implement the approved waste management plan.	The Board reviewed the status and considered the recommendation to be under implementation.		X			
62	2014	83	The Board recommended that UNRWA establish a mechanism, such as a project appraisal committee, to ensure that project risk assessments are conducted and included in project proposals, as required by the UNRWA project procedures manual (2011).	UNRWA management at the Lebanon field office agrees with the recommendation that project proposals include risk assessment and that mechanisms are established for accurate cost estimates. The Agency would like to highlight the fact that the issue is already being addressed through the formation of a project appraisal committee, comprising members of management, representatives of relevant departments and the Project Support Office and Donor Relations Unit. The committee is responsible for reviewing all proposals before they are submitted to donors and ensures that projects are based on identified needs and take into account all factors such as synergies with existing projects and/or programmes, support costs, including human resources requirements and risk	The Board reviewed the minutes of the meetings of the project appraisal committee and is satisfied with its review of the project proposals. In addition, in its assessment during the interim audit in the Lebanon field office, the Board noted improvement as the possible risks are considered in the project proposal.	X				

No.	Year of audit report	Paragraph reference	Board's recommendations	UNRWA response	Board's assessment	Implemented	Under implementation	Not implemented	Overtaken by events	Reiterated
				management. The Project Support Office is continuing to further develop a robust project appraisal process, which will further assist in ensuring smooth project implementation.						
63	2014	87	The Board reiterated its previous audit recommendation that UNRWA expedite the planned initiatives to reduce the length of the recruitment process by improving coordination within the hiring departments.	The post being referred to is the practical nurse post. During the recruitment process, there was a shift in the priorities as some posts are given a higher priority compared to other posts. The screening reviewed by the Board took longer than the time anticipated owing to the shift in priorities within the recruitment unit, where the Human Resources would have to balance available resources and the more urgent recruitment needs with a higher priority. Human Resources has exerted and will continue to exert and expedite its efforts to decrease the duration of the recruitment with weekly recruitment status updates on ongoing recruitments and follow-ups with the concerned departments. International vacancies are normally advertised for a period of one month. In rare instances, Human Resources may be requested to shorten the advertising period to three weeks, owing to urgency in filling a post given the unforeseen imminent departure of a staff member or	The Board considers the issue to be under implementation because UNRWA has to come up with appropriate measures to minimize deficiencies and workload in the recruitment sections.		X			

No.	Year of audit report	Paragraph reference	Board's recommendations	UNRWA response	Board's assessment	Implemented	Under implementation	Not implemented	Overtaken by events	Reiterated
				other arising resource gap. Human Resources considers the request and, where appropriate, shortens the advertising period to three weeks.						
64	2014	89	The Board recommended that UNRWA: (a) comply with the international staff selection policy on international staff recruitment to allow enough time to invite more applicants; and (b) ensure proper documentation in the recruitment files in cases where the recruitment policy is waived for the purpose of meeting the Agency's minimum operational requirements.	In this vein, the same considerations are applied when the required advertising period has been adjusted in the revised international staff selection policy I/104.2/Rev.3 (annex 1), which came into effect on 1 August 2014, stating in paragraph 25: "The Recruitment Section advertises the vacancy inviting candidates to apply through the Agency's e-recruitment system. Vacancies advertised targeting managed reassignment, internal and rostered candidates are to be advertised for 2 weeks. Vacancies not filled through an internal only process will normally be advertised internally and externally for 3 to 4 weeks. Exceptions, requesting shorter advertisement duration, will need to be approved by the Chief of the Human Resources Services Division and documented accordingly".	The recommendation has been implemented as all applications for waiver are now approved by the Chief of the Human Resources Services Division and documented accordingly.	X				

No.	Year of audit report	Paragraph reference	Board's recommendations	UNRWA response	Board's assessment	Implemented	Under implementation	Not implemented	Overtaken by events	Reiterated
65	2014	90	The Board recommended that UNRWA comply with staff selection policies and, that, where there is an exceptional case beyond the Agency's control, it document the reasons for extension to support its decision.	The special approvals to extend the rosters are an internal arrangement to respond to an immediate need to fill posts, and were obtained in a few cases where rosters were frozen for most of the actual roster period. UNRWA will minimize the use of such special approvals. Also in line with personnel directive No. 4 for Area staff regarding roster management: "the roster for candidates who were approved to be suitable to filling vacancies but not selected shall be placed on the roster of pre-approved candidates for up to one year". However, given the difficult circumstances that UNRWA faces, such as regarding the continuity of funding for core programmes, one-time exceptional approvals to extend the rosters were granted for two categories of post: (1) sanitation labourers/ school attendants (owing to the recruitment freeze); and (2) teachers (owing to the late receipt of government clearance). The field office considers the audit recommendation to be closed.	The special approval referred to in the management response has not yet been made available to the Board. Therefore, the recommendation is categorized as under implementation.		X			
66	2014	92	The Board recommended that UNRWA update the disaster recovery plan in order to: (a) accommodate the critical systems of the	The capabilities of the outsourced data centre, in the case of UNRWA, the Global Service Centre, are evolving. Historically the United Nations Logistics Base at Brindisi, Italy, was the only	This recommendation is implemented because the contract has been signed and the disaster recovery plan has been reviewed.	X				

No	Year of audit report	Paragraph reference	Board's recommendations	UNRWA response	Board's assessment	Implemented	Under implementation	Not implemented	Overtaken by events	Reiterated
			outsourced data centre; and (b) expedite signing of the contract with the vendor hosting the new enterprise resource planning system and Citrix.	outsourced data centre. Later, the requirements to expand data centres emerged. Capacity of the Global Service Centre has recently been expanded, with the establishment of a secondary active telecommunications facility in Valencia, Spain. The enterprise resource planning system is hosted in Valencia with backup capability provided in Brindisi. UNRWA intends to restructure its older systems currently hosted only in Brindisi so as to allow redundant backup from either Valencia or Brindisi. New systems in development (for example, the Education Management Information System) will have a backup data centre in place from their inception. The Disaster Recovery Plan will be updated accordingly.						
67	2014	93	The Board recommended that UNRWA: (a) review the backup policy and procedures for user access to reflect the new requirements of the enterprise resource planning system; (b) expedite the customization of the service desk express application to accommodate the handling of incidents arising from the	The capabilities of the outsourced data centre, in the case of UNRWA, the Global Service Centre, are evolving. Historically the United Nations Logistics Base at Brindisi, Italy, was the only outsourced data centre. Later, the requirements to expand data centres emerged. Capacity of the Global Service Centre has recently been expanded, with the establishment of a secondary active telecommunications facility in Valencia, Spain.	There is technology set up for replication between Brindisi and Valencia. However, the existing backup policy does not reflect the new enterprise resource planning system and there were no procedures for the provision of new users' access incorporated in the new enterprise resource planning		X			

No.	Year of audit report	Paragraph reference	Board's recommendations	UNRWA response	Board's assessment	Implemented	Under implementation	Not implemented	Overtaken by events	Reiterated
			implementation of the new system and train service desk staff accordingly, before the system becomes fully operational; and (c) develop project closure plans for the system to ensure its smooth transition from the project to the operational stage.	The enterprise resource planning system is hosted in Valencia with backup capability provided in Brindisi. UNRWA intends to restructure its older systems currently hosted only in Brindisi so as to allow redundant backup from either Valencia or Brindisi. New systems in development (for example, the Education Management Information System) will have a backup data centre in place from their inception. The Disaster Recovery Plan will be updated accordingly.	system. The recommendation is still under implementation					
68	2014	96	The Board recommended that UNRWA: (a) review the information security policy to cover the security issues posed by mobile devices; and (b) develop mobile device security guidelines and create awareness among users.	UNRWA believes that access to its main applications via telephone or wireless networks is adequately provided for using existing application access controls that require normal user identification and password controls. The Agency agrees that an area of vulnerability comes with the potential loss or theft of mobile devices. To that end, UNRWA will update its security policies in respect of actions to be taken should such events occur and communicate this guidance in due course.	A draft of the updated policy has been prepared and is awaiting approval. The issue is considered to be under implementation.		X			
69	2014	102	The Board recommended that UNRWA: (a) expedite the automation of the follow-up system for internal audit recommendations in	An action tracking system is now in place to record and monitor Department of Internal Oversight Services recommendations in the results-based management system. The new tracking	The recommendation is considered to be implemented because the tracking system is in place and working.	X				

No.	Year of audit report	Paragraph reference	Board's recommendations	UNRWA response	Board's assessment	Implemented	Under implementation	Not implemented	Overtaken by events	Reiterated
			the results-based management action tracking system to ensure the efficient and effective tracking of the recommendations of the Department of Internal Oversight Services; and (b) ensure that the experience gained from the pilot test of the action tracking system at the Jordan field office is well documented for future use during the expansion to other fields, in order to make it cost-effective.	system is now being used by the Department of Internal Oversight Services and the Jordan field office is piloting the new system, and progress is being documented.						
70	2014	107	The Board recommended that UNRWA: (a) ensure that intake committees are established at all field offices to review allegations of misconduct for quality assurance; and (b) consider developing a policy that will guide the reporting of investigation activities conducted by staff at the field offices and by headquarters departments.	Part (a) intake committees have been established in all field offices; and part (b) the 2010 Department of Internal Oversight Services guide for conducting investigations contains developments on the reporting of investigation activities. Part (a) has already been completed and is now part of the loan application procedure.	The Board has reviewed the appointment letters and meeting minutes and the Department of Internal Oversight Services guide for conducting investigations, therefore the Board considers this recommendation as implemented.	X				

No.	Year of audit report	Paragraph reference	Board's recommendations	UNRWA response	Board's assessment	Implemented	Under implementation	Not implemented	Overtaken by events	Reiterated
71	2014	113	The Board reiterated its recommendations that the Microfinance Department: (a) improve controls by establishing an online loan application process in the new Omni enterprise system in 2015; (b) closely supervise cashiers' activities, offer training and instruct cashiers to strictly follow operational procedures, including updating the cheque register, which is to be verified on a quarterly basis by branch managers; and (c) adopt proper follow-up procedures for all borrowers, focusing on those with late payments, while adhering to the agreed terms and conditions during loan disbursement.	Part (b) was completed and the procedural manual updated, staff trained on the correct procedures and increased supervision of the branches introduced to ensure compliance. Microfinance Department management issued instructions to cashiers to strictly adhere to cashiering functions and procedures, all Microfinance Department cashiers attended training sessions to improve their skills, all required forms were adjusted, new envelopes were printed, the cheque register was updated and the Department of Finance increased the number of field visits to cashiers. Part (c) Microfinance Department management issued instructions to branch managers to strictly adhere to follow-up procedures with late payment clients and print follow-up reports and document follow-up notes on time. Corrective actions taken by related branches and new follow-up reports were printed and follow-up actions were documented. As such, UNRWA considers corrective action to have been implemented.	The Board has reiterated the recommendation as the noted issues are still recurring.					X
Total					71	25	37	1	1	7
Percentage						36	52	1	1	10

Annex II

Summary of assets written off

(United States dollars)

Category	2015	2014	Increase/(decrease)
Cash	2 165	5 244	(3 079)
Inventory	25 513	456 000	(430 487)
Property	3 261 424	1 348 000	1 913 424
Outstanding contribution receivables	170 000	146 300	23 700
Outstanding loans receivables	809 527	860 000	(50 473)
Total	**4 268 629**	**2 815 544**	**1 453 085**

Source: UNRWA information.

Annex III

Ex gratia payments reported to the Board for the year 2015

Beneficiary name	Amount in United States dollars	Purpose of payment
Ghadeer Khalil Zaid	59 322	Death of her child at birth (asphyxia) at the Agency's Qalqilia Hospital
14 Agency staff in the Syrian Arab Republic	1 400	The special payment was paid to staff who worked during a snowstorm in a warehousing compound (each staff member took $100)
Yousef Hasan, Rawan Halaweh, Mohammad Khader	507	Medical treatment fees
Wafa'a Alfandaq, Isra'a Munawwar, Hasan Mheilan, Mohammad Ali and Omar Mostafa	500	Medical treatment for their daughters in Italy (pocket money $100 for each)
Total	**61 729**	

Annex IV

Cases of fraud and presumptive fraud reported to the Board for the year 2015

Case number	Office	Case type	Loss (United States dollars)	Description	Outcome
INV-13-0181	West Bank field office	General fraud	–	A staff member is alleged to have falsified their sick leave certificate.	Unable to substantiate
INV-14-0038	Gaza field office	Theft	The amount has not been determined	An UNRWA school principal reported the theft of diesel from a school generator.	Declined to investigate due to time elapsed
INV-14-0078	West Bank field office	General fraud	The amount has not been determined	It is alleged that several staff members may have misused Agency vehicles by recording private travel as duty travel.	Unsubstantiated
INV-14-0094	West Bank field office	General fraud	–	A staff member is alleged to have deceived the Agency by travelling outside the duty station during a period of sick leave.	Substantiated, referred for management intervention
INV-14-0095	West Bank field office	General fraud	–	A staff member is alleged to have deceived the Agency by travelling outside the duty station during a period of sick leave.	Substantiated, referred for management intervention
INV-14-0108	West Bank field office	General fraud	–	Alleged counterfeit of a staff member's UNRWA driving permit.	Recorded for information. Insufficient information to conduct the investigation
INV-14-0109	West Bank field office	Theft	116	A staff member is alleged to have stolen hospital materials.	Allegation of theft partially substantiated
INV-15-0002	Lebanon field office	General fraud	The amount has not been determined	False documents submitted in the course of a construction project, but owing to the security situation, the extent of the fraud and amounts involved could not be ascertained.	Substantiated — 4 staff members terminated
INV-15-0021	Lebanon field office	General fraud	–	Employee alleged to have submitted forged university certificate.	Unsubstantiated

Case number	Office	Case type	Loss (United States dollars)	Description	Outcome
INV-15-0032	Lebanon field office	General fraud	—	A staff member is alleged to have tricked a beneficiary family into giving him $6,632 to register their son in a Syrian embassy.	Unsubstantiated, the fraud was not against the Agency
INV-15-0037	Lebanon field office	Theft	The amount has not been determined	A staff member is alleged to have provided unauthorized access for use of an UNRWA generator by nearby shops.	Unsubstantiated
INV-15-0073	Headquarters, Amman	General fraud	8 600	A fuel supplier is alleged to have misrepresented quantities of fuel delivered to UNRWA.	Substantiated
INV-15-0098	Gaza field office	General fraud	The amount has not been determined	Allegations of fraudulent medical prescriptions of medications to family members by UNRWA health-care staff.	Partially substantiated
INV-15-0108	Gaza field office	General fraud	The amount has not been determined	Anonymous complaint alleging that one employee receives 10 per cent of the value of contracts and/or works obtained by certain suppliers.	Recorded for information. Lack of sufficient information to investigate
INV-15-0119	West Bank field office	Entitlement fraud	—	An employee is alleged to have misrepresented his support to a dependent in order to obtain dependency benefits he was not entitled to.	Not substantiated
INV-15-0128	Jordan field office	General fraud	944	A truck driver is alleged to have misrepresented the use of fuel.	Substantiated
INV-15-0129	Jordan field office	General fraud	—	A driver is alleged to have used an UNRWA vehicle for private reasons.	Unsubstantiated
INV-15-0137	Gaza field office	Theft	5 187	Theft of money deposited by businesses who were awarded the management of canteen facilities in UNRWA installations	Substantiated

Case number	Office	Case type	Loss (United States dollars)	Description	Outcome
INV-15-0327	Lebanon field office	General fraud	The amount has not been determined	An employee is alleged to have forged two vaccination cards for a beneficiary.	Unsubstantiated
Total			**14 847**		

Chapter III

Certification of the financial statements

Letter dated 31 March 2016 from the Director of Finance of the United Nations Relief and Works Agency for Palestine Refugees in the Near East addressed to the Chair of the Board of Auditors

Pursuant to financial regulations 11.4 and 12.1, I have the honour to submit the financial statements for the United Nations Relief and Works Agency for Palestine Refugees in the Near East for the year ended 31 December 2015.

I certify that all transactions have been properly recorded in the accounting records and properly reflected in the Agency's financial accounts and appended statements, which I hereby certify as accurate and representative of the Agency's operating activities and the financial state of affairs as at 31 December 2015.

(*Signed*) Shadi **El-Abed**
Director of Finance

Chapter IV
Financial report for the year ended 31 December 2015

A. Introduction

Statement of the Commissioner-General

1.   In accordance with regulations 11.2 and 11.4 of the Financial Regulations and Rules of the United Nations Relief and Works Agency for Palestine Refugees in the Near East, I have the honour to submit the financial statements of UNRWA for the year ended 31 December 2015, which I hereby approve. The financial statements have been prepared and certified as correct by the Director of Finance.

B. Financial and budget analysis

Summary

2.   The year 2015 has been another challenging one for UNRWA, its donors and its beneficiaries. The Agency continues to play an essential role in providing vital services for the well-being, human development and protection of more than 5 million registered persons and the amelioration of their plight, pending the just resolution of the question of Palestine refugees. Throughout 2015, UNRWA sustained its efforts to meet the needs of Palestine refugees across its five fields of operation, despite the challenges associated with the dramatic deterioration of the political and security environment, specifically, access problems in the West Bank, the continuing blockade of the Gaza Strip, the persistent armed conflict in the Syrian Arab Republic and the security concerns with which the Agency is faced on a daily basis.

3.   Notwithstanding the difficult financial climate, donors continued to provide strong support, with $1,178.7 million in contributions, allowing UNRWA to continue to provide assistance to beneficiaries and to address emergencies in the Gaza Strip and the Syrian Arab Republic.

4.   The financial statements have been prepared on the accrual basis of accounting, in accordance with the requirements of the International Public Sector Accounting Standards (IPSAS). Where IPSAS are silent concerning a specific matter, the appropriate International Financial Reporting Standard or International Accounting Standard is applied.

5.   The Agency completed the implementation of a new SAP enterprise resource planning system (known as REACH) during 2015 and all balances were migrated from the legacy system. The new enterprise resource planning system replaces the previous financial, supply chain and human resource and payroll systems, resulting in changes in various areas including a new Chart of Accounts, changes in programme reporting structure, funding classification, project accounting, grant management, business warehouse reporting, business process and consolidation and other processes, thereby improving the efficiency of the operations of the Agency.

6.   The previous biennial budget (for 2014-2015) was presented on a modified cash basis. As that basis differs from the accrual basis applied to the financial

statements, reconciliation between the budget and the cash flow statement is provided in accordance with the requirements of IPSAS.

Financial performance for 2015

7.   The Agency's total revenue and income for 2015 was $1,212.8 million, compared with total expenses of $1,333.8 million, resulting in a net shortfall of $121.0 million for 2015.

8.   Detailed information on the financial performance of each fund is contained in note 33 to the financial statements and is summarized in table IV.1.

Table IV.1

Summary financial performance by fund for the period ended 31 December 2015

(Millions of United States dollars)

	Unearmarked activities	Earmarked activities					
	Programme budget	Restricted funds	Microfinance Department	Emergency appeals	Projects	Inter-fund elimination	Total
Total revenues	639.1	16.1	9.6	418.3	180.3	(50.6)	1 212.8
Total expenses	766.7	18.5	9.2	418.8	171.1	(50.5)	1 333.8
Surplus/(deficit) for the year	**(127.6)**	**(2.4)**	**0.3**	**(0.5)**	**9.2**	**(0.1)**	**(121.0)**

9.   The programme budget, restricted funds, and the emergency appeal recorded deficits of $127.6 million, $2.4 million and $0.5 million, respectively.

10.   The Microfinance Department recorded a surplus of $0.3 million, and the projects funds recorded a surplus of $9.2 million, owing primarily to revenue recognized for projects against which expenses will be incurred in future periods.

Revenue analysis

11.   Cash contributions are the primary source of revenue for the Agency, providing more than 95 per cent ($1,162.3 million) of total revenue. In-kind contributions for earmarked activities (restricted funds, emergency appeals and projects) recognized under IPSAS were valued at $16.4 million. This is an important element, allowing the Agency to carry out its activities, and includes food and medical supplies, school textbooks, in-kind services for consultancy and project staff and the use of land for UNRWA facilities, such as schools and health clinics.

Figure IV.I
Revenue and income sources

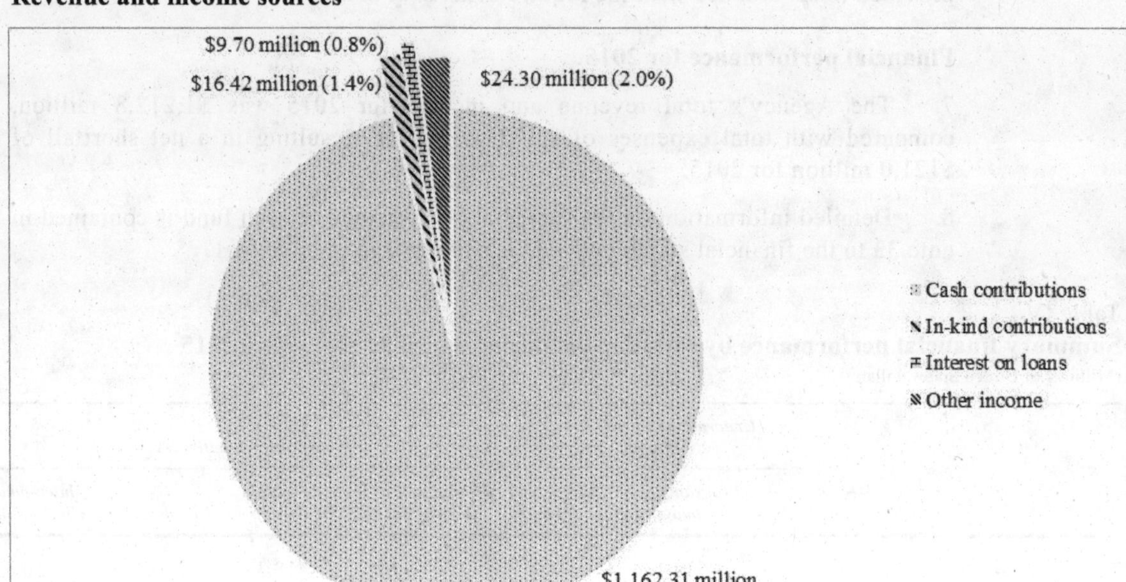

12. All key donors reaffirm their support every six months at a semi-annual meeting of the Advisory Commission. UNRWA is also widening its donor base, strengthening relationships with Arab donors, engaging new private partners and countries to build presence in emerging markets, while further deepening relations with traditional donors.

Nature of expense analysis

13. The Agency spent a total of $1,333.8 million in 2015. Staff costs of $709.9 million represented 53 per cent of total expenses. As already highlighted, accrual accounting for post-employment and other long-term employee benefits requires that the cost of the schemes be recorded as the benefits are earned by staff, rather than on a pay-as-you-go basis. This methodology allows the Agency to better account for the true cost of employing its staff on an annual basis.

Figure IV.II
Expense analysis by nature of expense

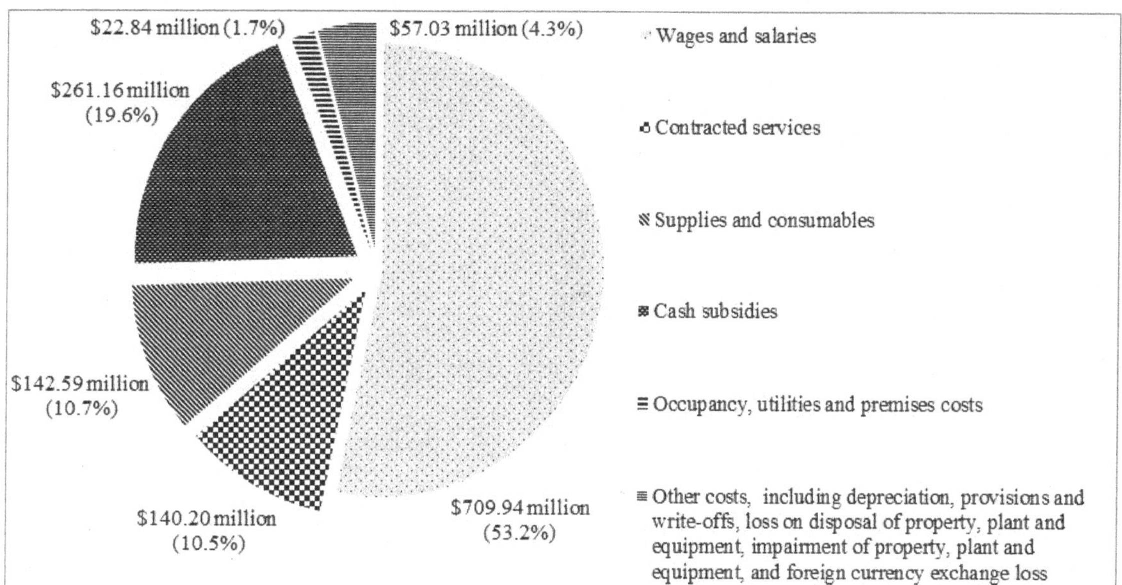

14. A total of $140.2 million was spent on contracted services, representing expenses relating to the Agency's engagement of third parties to perform work on its behalf. Of that amount, $49.4 million was spent on equipment and construction, which includes shelters and equipment that were donated to UNRWA beneficiaries and therefore expensed, as well as minor equipment for use by the Agency. A total of $28.4 million under the category of contracted services was spent on hospital services for the benefit of refugees.

15. A total of $142.6 million was spent on supplies and consumables, including $71.8 million for basic commodities and $13.6 million for fresh food. An amount of $23.6 million was spent on medical supplies, and $1.4 million was spent on text and library books. The sum of $9.0 million was spent on transportation supplies.

16. A total of $261.2 million was spent on subsidies, including $187.9 million distributed to beneficiaries providing selective cash assistance for conflict-affected Palestine refugees in the Syrian Arab Republic, food security and rent subsidies. The sum of $61.4 million was provided as subsidies for the construction and repair of shelters, and $5.8 million was provided for patient subsidies.

17. Occupancy and utility costs totalled $22.8 million in 2015. Other expenses, amounting to $57.0 million, included depreciation, provisions and write-offs, loss on disposal, impairment of fixed assets and foreign currency exchange loss.

Human development goals and Agency programmes: expense analysis

18. As part of its planning approach, UNRWA has four human development goals to provide it with direction in fulfilling its mission of helping Palestine refugees and the aim of accomplishing the goals with efficient and effective governance. The goals are (a) a long and healthy life; (b) acquired knowledge and skills; (c) a decent

standard of living; and (d) human rights enjoyed to the fullest. The amounts spent on each are shown in figure IV.III.

Figure IV.III
Expense analysis by human development goal[a]
(Millions of United States dollars)

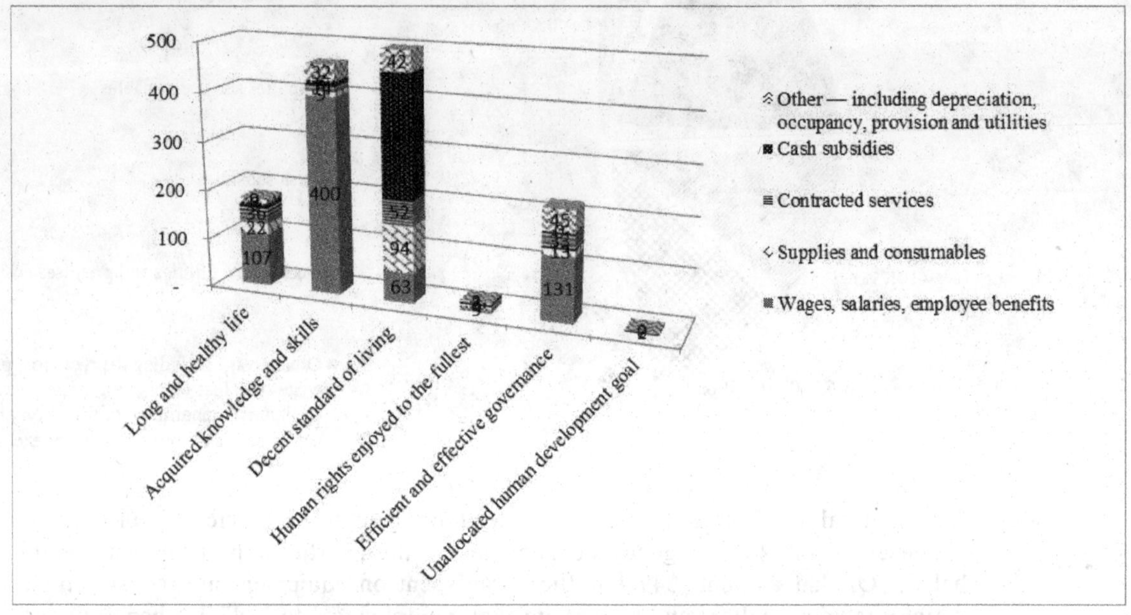

[a] 50.5 million in inter-segment eliminations are excluded from the analysis.

19. The Agency is functionally organized under four core programmes that provide direct services to UNRWA beneficiaries, led by executive direction and supported by support departments. Figure IV.IV below shows the 2015 expenses by programme and expenses for executive direction and support departments. The programmes follow a similar expense profile to those categorized by human development goal.

20. The objectives of the human development goal of a long and healthy life are to ensure universal access to quality comprehensive primary health care, protect and promote family health, and prevent and control diseases. An amount of $179.9 million (13 per cent of the Agency's total expenses) was spent in pursuit of this goal, which is supported through the health programme ($149.4 million). Approximately 59 per cent ($106.6 million) of the expenses dedicated to pursuing this goal was spent on wages and salaries, with 12 per cent ($22.3 million) spent on medical supplies and consumables and 20 per cent ($36.2 million) on contracted services to enable Palestine refugees to gain access to health-care services and to support the environmental health subprogramme. An additional 3 per cent ($6.1 million) was spent on cash subsidies to further enable Palestine refugees to gain access to secondary and tertiary health-care services.

21. The amount of $461.7 million, representing 33 per cent of the Agency's 2015 expenses, was spent on the goal of acquired knowledge and skills and delivered through the education programme ($512.8 million). The objectives are to ensure universal access to and coverage of basic education, enhance education quality and outcomes against set standards, and improve access to education opportunities for

learners with special education needs. The education programme also provides vocational and technical training and encourages the progression of students to higher education through scholarships. Given the nature of the programme and goal, the vast majority of the expenses in this area is spent on educational staff wages and salaries.

Figure IV.IV
Expense analysis by programme[a]
(Millions of United States dollars)

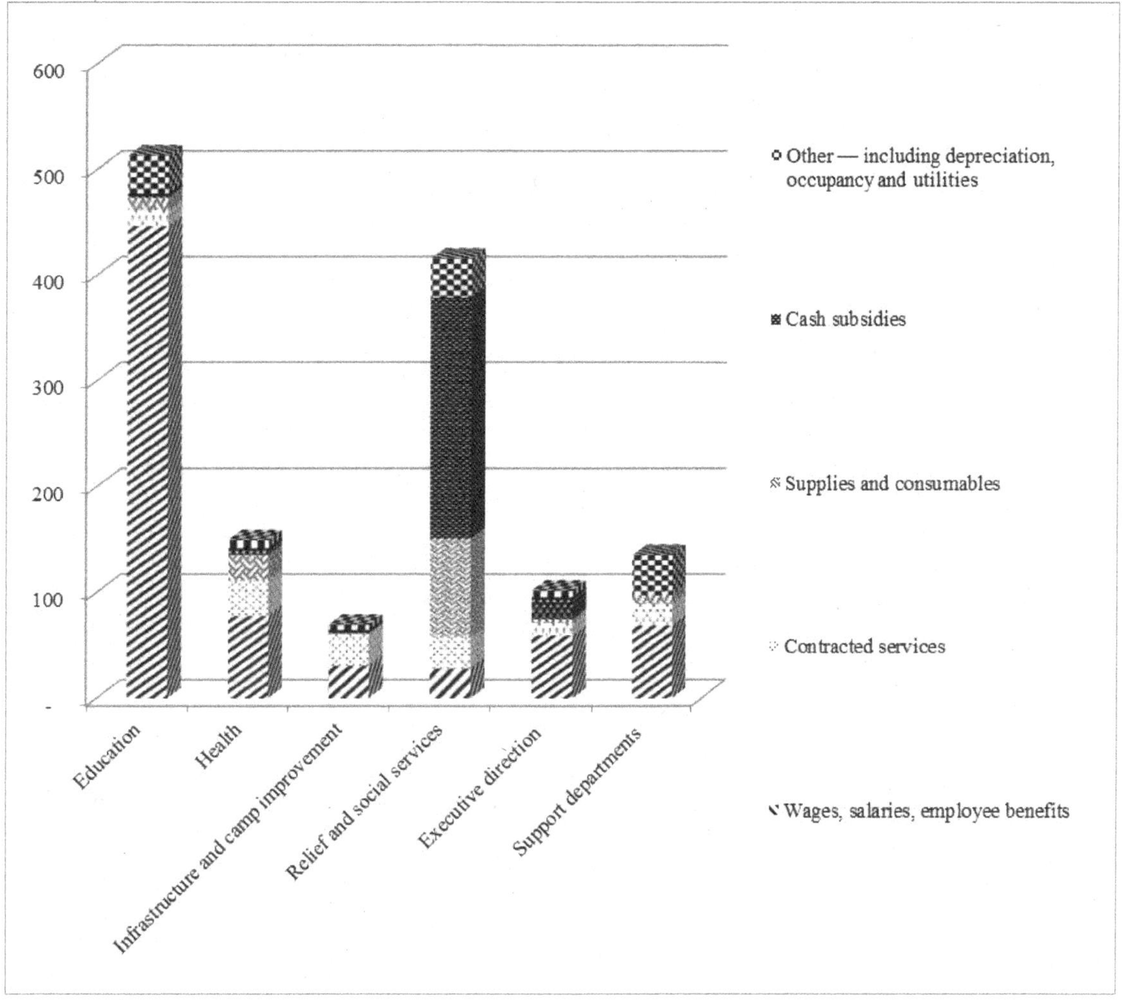

[a] $50.5 million in inter-segment eliminations are excluded from the analysis.

22. An amount of $498.1 million, or 36 per cent of UNRWA expenses, supported the human development goal of a decent standard of living, delivered largely through the relief and social services and infrastructure and camp improvement programmes ($415.1 million and $69.6 million, respectively). The objectives are to reduce abject poverty, mitigate the effects of emergencies on individuals, offer inclusive financial services and increased access to credit and savings facilities, improve employability and improve the urban environment. Nineteen per cent of the expenses ($94.2 million) dedicated to the pursuit of this goal was spent on supplies

and consumables, including the provision of food aid for Palestine refugees. An additional $246.9 million was provided in the form of cash subsidies.

23.   An amount of $222.1 million, or 17 per cent of the Agency's 2015 expenses, enables effective and efficient governance, which supports the activities to accomplish the four human development goals. Executive direction manages all aspects of the Agency's work to ensure efficient implementation of UNRWA mandates to provide services and humanitarian assistance to Palestine refugees, and to non-refugees on an exceptional basis, and to maintain the commitment of the international community to the social and economic well-being of Palestine refugees. Executive direction responsibilities include the effective management of oversight, legal support, fundraising, advocacy and outreach to external interlocutors.

24.   The support departments assist the Commissioner-General in the smooth running of the Agency and ensure effective management of personnel and financial resources, administrative services and internal communication. Expenses for executive direction and support departments amounted to $101.8 million and $135.3 million, respectively. Fifty-nine per cent of the expenses for effective and efficient governance ($131.3 million) was spent on wages and salaries.

25.   An amount of $20.1 million was spent on the human development goal of human rights enjoyed to the fullest extent possible. Objectives include ensuring that service delivery meets the protection needs of beneficiaries, safeguarding and advancing the rights of Palestine refugees, strengthening the capacity of refugees to formulate and implement sustainable social services in their communities, and ensuring that Palestine refugee registration and determination of eligibility for UNRWA services are carried out in accordance with relevant international standards. The services provided for the achievement of those objectives are delivered largely through the relief and social services programme, along with the services provided to achieve the objectives of the human development goal of a decent standard of living.

Geographical location: expense analysis

26.   Although UNRWA goals and services are delivered primarily within a programme approach, its operations are managed on a field basis. UNRWA operates in five fields: Jordan, Lebanon, the Syrian Arab Republic and the Occupied Palestinian Territory (the West Bank, including East Jerusalem, and the Gaza Strip). Each field provides similar services, but is distinctive to some extent owing to the particular political, humanitarian and economic contexts in which the field operates and the status and rights of the Palestine refugees enjoyed in it. Figure IV.V shows the costs of UNRWA services per refugee for each field. The different levels of expenses reflect the situations prevailing in each of the fields.

27.   The average 2015 expense per refugee in the Gaza field office is $452. The Gaza Strip has a population of more than 1.8 million, including some 1,311,920 registered Palestine refugees. The Agency's work continued to be affected during the past year by the consequences, including the extensive physical damage and destruction, of the 50-day conflict which took place during July and August 2014. Additionally, operations continued to be burdened by the direct costs of the ongoing blockade, such as additional staffing, transit and logistical costs as a result of Israeli requirements regarding access and monitoring of the materials the Agency imports

into the Gaza Strip, resulting in the highest average expense for the Agency per refugee in the field, which reflects the prevailing conditions.

28. UNRWA continues its efforts to provide relief, education, health and other human development services in the aftermath of the conflict and deteriorating socioeconomic conditions after almost nine years of blockade. The Gaza field office supports eight camps, 257 schools, two vocational and technical training centres, 22 primary health centres, seven community rehabilitation centres and seven women's programme centres.

29. The Lebanon field office has the lowest number of registered refugees, at just over 458,360, and the average expense per refugee is $420. Palestine refugees do not enjoy several basic human rights (e.g. they have restricted access to the local labour market) and many live in UNRWA refugee camps. The field office supports 12 camps, 67 schools, two vocational and technical training centres, one rehabilitation centre, 27 primary health centres, and eight women's programme centres.

Figure IV.V
Average 2015 expenses per registered refugee, by field[a]
(Millions of United States dollars)

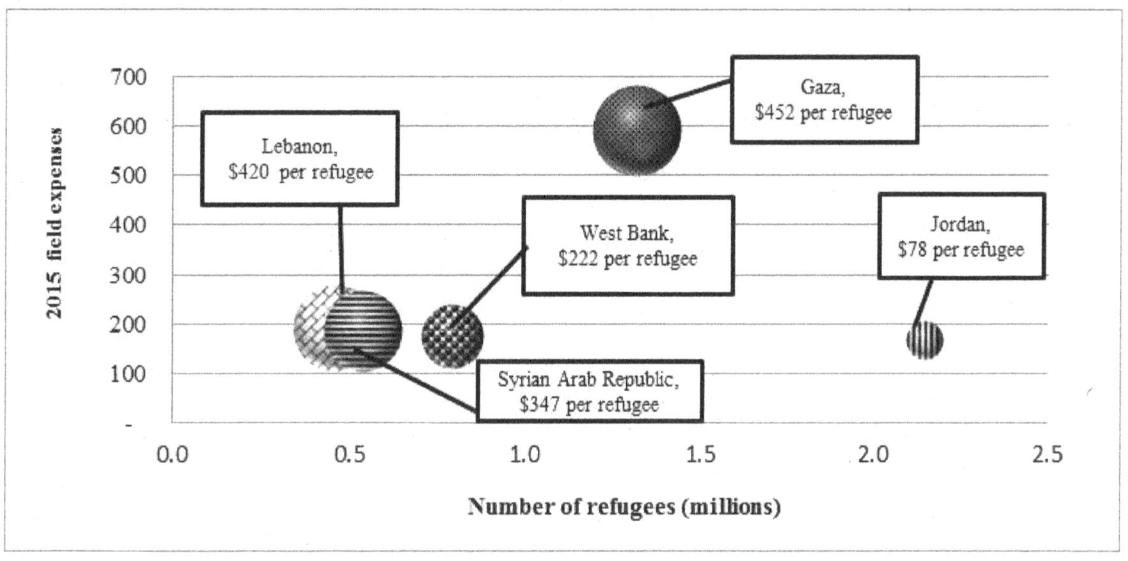

[a] $69.6 million in headquarters expenses and $50.5 million in inter-segment eliminations are excluded from the analysis.

30. The West Bank field office serves more than 792, registered Palestine refugees, with one quarter of them living in 19 refugee camps. West Bank refugees have been hard hit by closures imposed on the West Bank by the Israeli authorities, as historically they have been largely dependent on income from work inside Israel. The average 2015 expense per registered refugee in the West Bank is $222. In addition to the 19 camps, the field office supports 96 schools, two vocational and technical training centres, 43 primary health centres, 15 community rehabilitation centres and 18 women's programme centres.

31. The Syrian Arab Republic field office is mandated to provide services to nearly 534,660 Palestine refugees living in the official camps and the three unofficial camps

in the Syrian Arab Republic. The average 2015 expense per registered refugee is $347. The incessant armed conflict in the Syrian Arab Republic has affected the economy, thus impacting the Palestine refugee community. The field office supports nine camps, 100 schools, the Damascus Training Centre, 26 primary health centres, five community rehabilitation centres and 12 women's programme centres.

32. Over 2,144,230 Palestine refugees are registered in Jordan. All Palestine refugees in Jordan have full citizenship, with the exception of some 140,000 refugees originally from Gaza, who are eligible for temporary passports but are not entitled to vote or to work in government. The lowest average 2015 expense per refugee, at $78, reflects the situation of Palestine refugees living in Jordan. The field office supports 10 camps, 172 schools, two vocational and technical training centres, 25 primary health centres, eight community rehabilitation centres and 12 women's programme centres.

Financial position at the end of 2015

33. The Agency's net assets/equity decreased from $328.7 (restated) at 31 December 2014 to $196.1 million as at 31 December 2015.

34. The financial position of each fund is detailed in note 33 to the financial statements and is summarized in table IV.2.

Table IV.2
Summary financial position by fund as at 31 December 2015
(Millions of United States dollars)

	Unearmarked activities	Earmarked activities					
	Programme budget	Restricted funds	Microfinance Department	Emergency appeals	Projects	Inter-fund elimination	Total
Current assets	105.7	6.7	30.8	232.6	149.5	(6.8)	518.5
Non-current assets	459.6	2.0	3.1	1.0	39.2	–	504.0
Total assets	**565.3**	**8.7**	**33.9**	**233.6**	**188.7**	**(6.8)**	**1 023.4**
Current liabilities	162.4	0.9	1.6	25.8	13.4	(6.8)	197.3
Non-current liabilities	616.6	–	13.4	–	–	–	630.0
Total liabilities	**779.0**	**0.9**	**15.0**	**25.8**	**13.4**	**(6.8)**	**827.3**
Net assets/equity	**(213.7)**	**7.8**	**18.9**	**207.8**	**175.3**	**0.0**	**196.1**

35. The negative net assets/equity position of the programme budget is due primarily to the significant post-employment benefits liabilities, which was recognized in the financial statements upon adoption of IPSAS.

36. The net assets/equity balance of the projects fund showed a balance of $175.3 million, due primarily to contributions received or pledged for specific projects against which expenses are expected to be incurred in future years.

37. Net assets/equity is divided into fund balances of $191.4 million and reserves of $4.7 million.

38.   Although there is a negative net current asset balance for the programme budget, the net current assets (current assets less current liabilities) of the Agency were $321.2 million as at 31 December 2015 (compared with $349.4 million as at 31 December 2014), indicating positive short-term liquidity. The Agency's current assets amount to 51 per cent of its total assets, whereas current liabilities constitute 24 per cent of total liabilities.

Cash, cash equivalents and investments

39.   Total cash amounted to $308.8 million as at 31 December 2015, covering four to five months of operations (based on average monthly cash outflows in 2015). UNRWA holds short-term investments (bank deposits) which are classified as cash and cash equivalents.

Receivables

40.   Contributions receivable represent confirmed pledges outstanding from donors that are due within 12 months and were valued, net of provision for estimated reductions in contribution revenue and doubtful accounts, at $39.6 million as at 31 December 2015, owing primarily to projects ($29.6 million) and emergency appeals ($7.4 million).

41.   Accounts receivable, net of provision, were valued at $33.8 million as at 31 December 2015. This amount relates primarily to significant value-added tax refund claims of $104.6 million before provision, which are still due to the Agency for services and goods procured for the West Bank and the Gaza Strip, as well as $3.2 million related to personal accounts of UNRWA staff members. Loans receivable, net of provision, were valued at $26.1 million and relate to loans from the Microfinance Department and the microcredit community support programme. Of this amount, $22.7 million relates to short-term (current) loans receivable.

Inventories

42.   The value of the Agency's inventory at the end of 2015 was estimated at $101.9 million, reflecting an increase of $5.5 million compared with 31 December 2014. Assets included shelters under construction ($23.3 million), non-Agency installations ($11.5 million) and warehouse inventory ($45.0 million), as well as inventory in transit valued at $4.4 million, consisting of medical supplies, food, motor transport and general supplies to be distributed to Palestine refugees. Pharmacy/health clinic inventory was valued at $17.6 million, and production unit inventory for the embroidery centre located in the Gaza Strip was valued at $0.2 million.

Property, plant and equipment

43.   The total net carrying amount of property, plant and equipment as at 31 December 2015 was $464.8 million, representing 45 per cent of total Agency assets. This item is composed mainly of buildings used for the provision of services to UNRWA beneficiaries.

Figure IV.VI
Property, plant and equipment

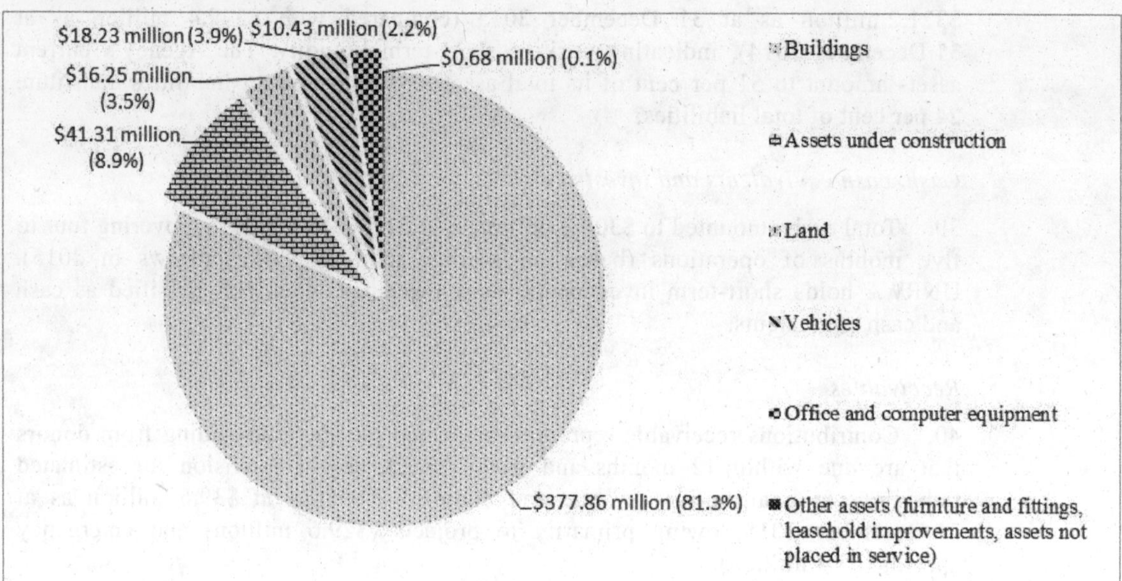

44.   Assets under construction amounted to $41.3 million as at 31 December 2015, relating largely to specific construction projects under the restricted funds and projects segments. Upon the completion of capital projects using earmarked funds, assets are transferred to the programme budget for use in the delivery of the Agency's core services to Palestine refugees.

45.   Land was valued at $16.3 million as at 31 December 2015. This figure appears relatively low because host Governments and some charitable organizations provide the use of land for no or nominal rent to UNRWA for the benefit of Palestine refugees. The leases under these contracts have been assessed as operating leases, and therefore such land is not included in the UNRWA balance sheet.

Employee benefits liabilities

46.   The Agency has significant liabilities relating to post-employment and other long-term employee benefits. Those liabilities amounted to $697.4 million as at the end of 2015, reflecting an increase of $137.2 million during the year. The employee benefits liabilities represent 84.3 per cent of the Agency's liabilities, with $77.4 million categorized as current liabilities and $620.1 million as non-current liabilities. Actuarial valuations have been used for termination and separation costs, employee disability and death-in-service benefits, accumulated annual leave, after-service health insurance and repatriation benefits. The increase during the year is primarily due to the change in the discount rate from 4.75 per cent to 4.32 per cent as per the continuous low interest rate environment ($29.0 million), the inclusion of the currency adjustment factor for basic salary in the Gaza Strip and West Bank ($40.2 million) and an increase in end-of-service benefits from 11 per cent to 12 per cent ($18.0 million).

47.   During the year the agency introduced the new exceptional voluntary separation scheme for Area staff under Area Staff Rule No. 109.15 and approximately

$12 million were paid during the year under the scheme. Eligibility is primarily extended to staff who occupy posts that the Agency may consider to be non-essential, staff who occupy posts in the education programme who lack the necessary professional qualifications and experience required for such posts and staff who qualify for early voluntary retirement.

Budgetary analysis

Basis of the budget

48.   The budget figures for UNRWA are determined on a modified cash basis and disclosed in the statement of comparison of budget and actual amounts (statement V) as the original budget derived from the 2014-2015 programme budget (Blue Book). The budget for UNRWA includes the core requirements funded through the programme budget (previously called General Fund), which, if exceeded requires submission to the General Assembly; and an in-kind donation budget and a projects budget, where allocation varies based on donor response.

Explanation of material differences

49.   The 2015 programme budget, projects budget and in-kind donation budget, as reflected in the Blue Book for 2014-2015, amounted to $982.2 million (on a modified cash basis). This is disclosed in financial statement V as "original" budget. The final 2015 programme budget was $1,083.3 million and is disclosed in financial statement V as "final" budget accordingly. The increase of $101.1 million, or 10.3 per cent, is primarily due to an increase in the final projects budget.

C.   Enhancing transparency and accountability

50.   Financial regulation 5.2 requires that the Commissioner-General of UNRWA maintain a system of internal controls to provide for an effective current examination or review of financial transactions to ensure the regularity of the receipt, custody and disposal of the resources of the Agency, to ensure the conformity of all expenses with the provisions of the Financial Regulations, and to detect any uneconomic use of the resources of the Agency.

51.   The Agency has a system of internal controls that are intended to safeguard assets, ensure adherence to regulations and rules, including management policies and procedures, and prevent fraud. To enhance transparency and control and ensure that no single individual has the final say in decisions, most high-level managerial responsibilities and decisions are administered by committees. The Agency has established detailed instructions and procedures to ensure effective financial administration and the exercise of economy. There are also organizational directives to guide the day-to-day running of the Agency and ensure adherence to internal controls.

52.   In addition, the annual workplan of the Department of Internal Oversight Services includes reviews of the Agency's system of internal controls and makes recommendations for improvements. The Department's workplan and resulting reports are considered by the Agency's independent external oversight body, the Advisory Committee on Internal Oversight, which provides advice on this and financial accountability in general to the Commissioner-General.

53. Furthermore, since 2010, monthly financial reports have been issued to the members of the Management Committee of UNRWA and to major donors. This has increased transparency both internally and externally. The reports to senior management have served to strengthen its focus on identified financial risks.

D. Enterprise and financial risk management

Enterprise risk management

54. A broad spectrum of risks is associated with the existence and the operations of UNRWA. The risks fall mainly in the broad categories of operational, environmental and financial risk. The management of risks is aimed at reducing the Agency's exposure to various forms of loss and, more critically, to shortcomings in the delivery of services to the Palestine refugees in the areas of education, health, relief and social services, and infrastructure and camp improvement.

55. "Operational risk" refers mainly to the risk of failing to deliver the services for which, according to its mandate, the Agency exists. Such risk is managed through proper planning, control and performance reviews and evaluations in the Agency's main areas of operation (education, health, relief and social services, and infrastructure and camp improvement).

56. Operational risk is also managed at the field level because, although the five fields in which UNRWA operates share similarities, they are also distinctive. In recognition of this, in 2009, responsibility for the delivery of services to UNRWA beneficiaries was devolved to the fields. While guided by the Agency's goals and programmes of priority services, this devolution to operational fields has provided greater discretion to field offices in the provision of services geared towards local needs, taking into account the realities in the field and the field's available resources. Such devolution, along with centralized policymaking and the regular monitoring of results, provides for enhanced management of the Agency's operational risk.

57. "Environmental risk" is the inherent risk associated with the volatile nature of the environment in which the Agency operates. Such risk is managed through recognition of the potential danger and the political and security concerns posed by the conflicts in the greater Middle East, particularly in the areas in which the Agency operates: Jordan, the Syrian Arab Republic, Lebanon, the West Bank and the Gaza Strip. The security alerts are set at the appropriate levels, and all risk-mitigating elements are installed and monitored on an ongoing basis.

Financial risk management

58. The Agency is prone to exposure to various forms of financial risk, the greatest of which is the risk of failure to have sufficient financial resources to achieve the planned objectives and activities. The source of funding for operations aimed at meeting the objectives of the Agency and the needs of the refugees is predominantly the donor community. The uncertainty surrounding the timing and the actual amounts of voluntary contributions also poses some financial risk when it comes to planning. Such risk is managed in the best way possible by considering the available information and providing for inflows in the most prudent manner.

59. The Agency's activities expose it to various financial risks, primarily the effects of changes in foreign currency exchange rates, given that most contributions

are in currencies other than the Agency's reporting currency, the United States dollar. Consequently, UNRWA financial risk management focuses on the unpredictability of foreign exchange rates and seeks to minimize, where feasible, potential adverse effects on the Agency's financial performance. Financial risk management is carried out by a central treasury function using UNRWA technical guidelines covering areas of financial risk, such as foreign exchange, the use of derivative financial instruments and the investment of excess liquidity. There is no perceived risk that receivables and payables will not be liquidated when they fall due.

60. The Agency's employee benefits liabilities totalled $697.4 million as at 31 December 2015. UNRWA has sought advice from independent actuaries in establishing the value of those liabilities. The funding of employee benefits liabilities remains a long-term risk for the Agency. UNRWA adopts a pay-as-you-go method and the cash to be paid for the coming year is planned and budgeted. For the long-term portion of the liabilities, the matter is inherently tied to the nature of UNRWA and its temporary mandate. It is fully expected that when there is a sustainable political solution resolving the displacement of Palestine refugees, this solution will address, among other matters, the future of UNRWA activities along with the dissolution of its assets and liabilities.

E. Responsibility

61. In accordance with regulations 11.2 and 11.4 of the Financial Regulations and Rules of UNRWA, I am pleased to submit the Agency's financial statements, which have been prepared under IPSAS (see chap. V). The financial statements have been certified as correct by the Director of Finance.

Chapter V

Financial statements for the year ended 31 December 2015

United Nations Relief and Works Agency for Palestine Refugees in the Near East

I. Statement of financial position as at 31 December 2015

(Thousands of United States dollars)

	Reference	31 December 2015	31 December 2014 (restated)
Assets			
Current assets			
Cash and cash equivalents	Note 4	308 784	305 454
Short-term loans receivable	Note 5	22 685	21 178
Contributions receivable	Note 6	39 639	38 188
Accounts receivable	Note 7	33 769	42 607
Other current assets	Note 8	4 058	7 241
Inventories	Note 3, 9	101 908	96 361
Derivative financial assets	Note 10	7 658	4 877
Non-current assets			
Other non-current assets	Note 8	188	234
Long-term loans receivable	Note 5	3 408	2 594
Property, plant and equipment	Note 11	464 778	449 985
Intangible assets	Note 12	36 526	31 160
Total assets		**1 023 401**	**999 879**
Liabilities			
Current liabilities			
Payables and accruals	Note 13	67 293	86 551
Employee benefits	Note 14, 15	77 350	65 482
Derivative financial liabilities	Note 10	1 085	6 755
Other current liabilities	Note 16	5 438	5 145
Advance contributions	Note 17	46 170	2 608
Non-current liabilities			
Employee benefits	Note 14, 15	620 087	494 786
Other non-current liabilities	Note 13	9 875	9 875
Total liabilities		**827 298**	**671 202**
Net assets		**196 103**	**328 677**
Net assets/equity			
Revaluation and Other reserves		(23 022)	(11 302)
Capital reserve: microcredit community support programme and Microfinance Department	Note 19	27 753	27 562
Accumulated surplus	Note 3	191 372	312 417
Total net assets/equity		**196 103**	**328 677**

United Nations Relief and Works Agency for Palestine Refugees in the Near East

II. Statement of financial performance for the year ended 31 December 2015

(Thousands of United States dollars)

	Reference	2015	2014 (restated)
Revenue			
Cash contributions	Note 20	1 162 308	1 292 525
In-kind contributions	Note 21	16 421	28 663
Interest on loans	Note 22	9 701	8 049
Interest on bank deposits	Note 23	344	453
Other revenue			
Foreign currency exchange gain	Note 24	4 713	–
Programme support cost recovery	Note 25	161	98
Financial derivative gain	Note 10	11 404	3 899
Miscellaneous revenue	Note 26	7 678	11 090
Total revenue		**1 212 730**	**1 344 777**
Expenses			
Wages, salaries and employee benefits	Note 27	709 941	651 500
Supplies and consumables	Note 28	142 593	186 027
Occupancy, utilities and premises costs	Note 29	22 841	21 968
Contracted services	Note 30	140 203	143 560
Subsidies	Note 31	261 164	235 711
Depreciation and amortization	Note 11, 12	30 324	24 578
Provision and write-offs	Note 32	23 343	19 458
Loss on disposal	Note 11	3 261	1 348
Impairment of property, plant and equipment	Note 11	104	593
Foreign currency exchange loss	Note 24	–	16 343
Total expenses		**1 333 775**	**1 301 085**
Surplus/(deficit) for the year		**(121 045)**	**43 692**

United Nations Relief and Works Agency for Palestine Refugees in the Near East

III. Statement of changes in net assets/equity for the year ended 31 December 2015

(Thousands of United States dollars)

	Revaluation and other reserve[a]	Reserves, microcredit community support programme and Microfinance Department	Accumulated surplus/deficit — unearmarked	Accumulated surplus/deficit — earmarked	Total
Balance at 1 January 2015	**(11 302)**	**27 562**	**(83 384)**	**387 190**	**320 066**
Prior year adjustment[b]	–	–	906	7 705	8 611
Balance at 1 January 2015 as restated	**(11 302)**	**27 562**	**(82 478)**	**394 895**	**328 677**
Changes in net assets/equity for 2015					
Reclassification of funds	–	–	19 956	(19 956)	–
Surplus/(deficit) for the period	–	–	(127 631)	6 586	(121 045)
Gain on revaluation of derivative financial instruments	8 450	–	–	–	8 450
Reserves, microcredit community support programme and Microfinance Department, during 2015	–	191	–	–	191
Actuarial (loss) on staff termination liabilities[c]	(20 170)	–	–	–	(20 170)
Total net assets/equity	**(23 022)**	**27 753**	**(190 153)**	**381 525**	**196 103**

[a] See note 33.
[b] See note 3.
[c] See note 15.12.

United Nations Relief and Works Agency for Palestine Refugees in the Near East

IV. Statement of cash flow for the year ended 31 December 2015

(Thousands of United States dollars)

	2015	*2014*
Cash flows from operating activities		
(Deficit)/surplus for the year	(121 045)	43 692
Adjustment for non-cash items		
Add depreciation and amortization	30 324	24 578
Loss on disposal	3 261	1 348
Impairment of property, plant and equipment	104	593
Actuarial gain/(loss) on employee benefit liabilities	(20 170)	2 269
Increase in provision for doubtful debts	22 283	17 993
(Increase)/decrease in inventories	(5 548)	6 442
(Increase) in contributions receivable	(5 554)	(15 074)
(Increase) in accounts receivable	(9 525)	(7 710)
(Increase) in loans receivable	(2 138)	(2 936)
Decrease in other assets	3 230	285
(Decrease) in accounts payable and accruals	(19 259)	(17 499)
Increase in leave encashment and employee benefits	137 169	33 711
Increase/(decrease) in other liabilities	294	(8 068)
Increase/(decrease) in advance contributions	43 562	(4 341)
Net cash from operating activities	**56 988**	**75 283**
Cash flows from investing activities		
Proceeds from sale of property, plant and equipment	8	150
Purchase of property, plant, equipment and adjustment	(43 330)	(33 734)
Purchase of intangible assets	(10 527)	(16 009)
Net cash from investing activities	**(53 849)**	**(49 593)**
Cash flows from financing activities		
Increase in capital reserve for Microfinance Department and microcredit community support programme	191	1 369
Net cash from financing activities	**191**	**1 369**
Net increase in cash	3 330	27 059
Cash balance at the beginning of the year	305 454	278 395
Cash balance at the end of the year	**308 784**	**305 454**

United Nations Relief and Works Agency for Palestine Refugees in the Near East

V. Statement of comparison of budget and actual amounts for the year ended 31 December 2015

(Thousands of United States dollars)

		Budget amounts		Actual on comparable basis	Variances: final budget and actual
	Reference	Original	Final		
Staff costs					
International staff		**30 798**	**40 957**	**36 499**	**4 458**
Area staff					
Basic salary		370 445	363 129	344 321	18 808
Hazard pay and special elements		–	255	205	50
Provident Fund Agency contribution		55 363	57 716	53 716	4 000
Special professional occupational allowance, special occupational allowance and others		10 946	11 451	11 982	(531)
Overtime and excess hours supplement		673	1 692	1 460	232
Currency adjustment factor		12 459	18 990	11 117	7 873
Special allowance		19 627	18 803	18 388	415
Health-related expenses		8 172	8 961	9 430	(469)
Other miscellaneous staff costs		302	117	178	(61)
Severance cash payment out		16 103	27 239	19 737	7 502
Limited duration contract		3 610	9 512	5 003	4 509
Temporary staff		7 411	19 932	16 484	3 448
Total staff costs (A)	Note 34	**535 909**	**578 754**	**528 520**	**50 234**
Non-staff costs					
Supplies		61 818	88 090	73 104	14 986
Utilities		7 121	6 125	5 854	271
Maintenance of premises		8 184	17 284	14 515	2 769
Equipment and non-capital construction		194 327	196 474	153 125	43 349
Training		5 895	5 359	3 026	2 333
Travel		1 992	3 558	2 658	900
Administrative support services		5 651	8 993	7 386	1 607
Consultancy services		2 537	16 951	12 900	4 051
Hospital services		20 579	20 011	19 654	357
Miscellaneous services		20 537	30 499	23 896	6 603
Subsidies to hardship cases		11 558	48 862	42 355	6 507
Subsidies to patients		5 297	5 728	4 911	817
Third-party subsidies		22 076	1 281	863	418
Other subsidies		362	19 592	11 744	7 848
Cost recovery		(3 109)	(12 658)	(4 899)	(7 759)
Reserves		81 444	48 354	–	48 354
Total non-staff costs (B)	Note 34	**446 269**	**504 503**	**371 092**	**133 411**
Total resources requirements (A+B)	Note 34	**982 178**	**1 083 257**	**899 612**	**183 645**

United Nations Relief and Works Agency for Palestine Refugees in the Near East

Notes to the 2015 financial statements

Note 1
Mission statement

The United Nations Relief and Works Agency for Palestine Refugees in the Near East (UNRWA or the Agency) is a United Nations agency established by the General Assembly in 1949 and is mandated to provide assistance and protection to a population of some 5 million registered Palestine refugees. Its mission is to help Palestine refugees in Jordan, Lebanon, the Syrian Arab Republic, the West Bank and the Gaza Strip to achieve their full potential in human development, pending a just solution to their plight. UNRWA services encompass education, health care, relief and social services, camp infrastructure and improvement, microfinance and emergency assistance. UNRWA is funded almost entirely by voluntary contributions.

Note 2
Summary of significant accounting policies

(a) Basis of presentation

2.1 The financial statements have been prepared on the accrual basis of accounting, in accordance with the requirements of the International Public Sector Accounting Standards (IPSAS). Where IPSAS are silent concerning any specific matter, the appropriate International Financial Reporting Standard or International Accounting Standard is applied.

2.2 There are currently no standards issued by the IPSAS Board awaiting implementation that would be likely to affect the financial statements of UNRWA.

(b) Accounting convention

2.3 The financial statements have been prepared using the historical cost convention, except for some financial instruments that are carried at fair value, and donated inventory or property, plant and equipment, which are valued at fair value.

(c) Functional currency and translation of foreign currencies

Functional and presentation currency

2.4 The financial statements are presented in United States dollars, and all values are rounded to the nearest thousand. The functional currency of the Agency is the United States dollar, with the exception of the Microfinance Department, which uses the Syrian pound as the functional currency in the Syrian Arab Republic and the Jordanian dinar as the functional currency in the West Bank and Jordan.

Transactions and balances

2.5 Foreign currency transactions are translated into United States dollars using the United Nations operational rates of exchange, which approximate the exchange rates prevailing at the dates of the transactions. The United Nations operational rates of exchange are set once a month and are revised mid-month if there are significant exchange rate fluctuations relating to individual currencies.

2.6 Monetary assets and liabilities denominated in foreign currencies are translated into United States dollars at the year-end closing rate of the United Nations operational rates of exchange.

2.7 Both realized and unrealized foreign exchange gains and losses resulting from the settlement of foreign currency transactions and from the translation, at year-end exchange rates, of monetary assets and liabilities denominated in foreign currencies are recognized in the statement of financial performance.

Management of currency risks

2.8 The primary principle of the currency risk management policy of UNRWA is the preservation of the value of its financial resources in United States dollar terms. The Agency's currency risk can be identified mainly as a potential loss in the value of non-received non-United States dollar contributions and non-United States dollar cash assets as a result of a strengthening United States dollar. The risk arises from the date on which the contributions are pledged. To protect its assets and cash flow against adverse currency movements, UNRWA adopts a conservative risk management approach (e.g. hedging) to minimize its exposure to exchange rate fluctuations. To hedge the currency risk, UNRWA entered into several forward contracts in 2015 for expected non-United States dollar programme budget contributions in 2016 (see note 10). In 2015, the Agency expanded the Investment Review Committee by including three external advisers to provide more professional expertise in cash and risk management.

2.9 Such hedges are consistent with the Agency's risk management objective and strategy, given that they remove the risk of an appreciation of the United States dollar and provide a fixed known income amount. The gain or loss from hedging will be offset by the foreign exchange gain or loss from donor contributions.

2.10 The Agency provides protection against volatility in local currencies (currency adjustment factor) to its area staff for their salaries. Its currency risk management policies allow hedging against local currencies to reduce exposure arising from fluctuations in exchange rates between the United States dollar and local currencies. At the end of the year, there were several outstanding hedging instruments for local currencies (see note 10).

(d) Materiality and use of judgment and estimates

2.11 Materiality is central to the Agency's financial statements. The Agency's accounting materiality framework provides a systematic method for identifying, analysing, evaluating, endorsing and periodically reviewing materiality decisions that affect a number of accounting areas.

2.12 The financial statements necessarily include amounts based on judgments, estimates and assumptions by management. Changes in estimates are reflected in the period during which they become known.

(e) Significant accounting policies

Cash and cash equivalents

2.13 Cash and cash equivalents include cash on hand, cash at banks and other short-term highly liquid investments with original maturities of two to three months.

Revenue

2.14 Revenue is recognized in the statement of financial performance when an increase in future economic benefits relating to an increase in an asset or a decrease in a liability has arisen from a mutually agreed interaction between two parties and can be measured reliably.

(i) Revenue from non-exchange transactions

Contributions are recognized in accordance with IPSAS 23, Income from non-exchange transactions. For unconditional contributions, revenue recognition occurs when the contributions are confirmed in writing by donors. However, if conditions requiring specific performance and the return of unexpended balances exist, then revenue is recognized upon provision of the goods and services. When projects come to an end, and in the event that some contributions are not fully expended on the project for which they were given, then at that point in time, and in accordance with the donor agreement, the amounts that will not be expended will be recognized as amounts to be refunded to donors and included in the statement of financial position and, as other income (expense), in the statement of financial performance. Contributions received from donors in advance are recorded as other liabilities in the statement of financial position until the criteria for recording revenue are met. Notes 20 and 21 provide further details of cash contributions revenue and in-kind contributions revenue, which are recognized in accordance with this policy.

(ii) Revenue from exchange transactions

Revenue from exchange transactions is recognized in accordance with IPSAS 9. When the amount of revenue can be measured reliably, it is probable that the economic benefits or service potential associated with the transaction will flow to the entity, the stage of completion of the transaction at the reporting date can be measured reliably and the costs incurred for the transaction and the costs to complete the transaction can be measured reliably.

Notes 22 to 26 give further details of revenue earned from exchange transactions, which is brought to account in accordance with this policy. This includes revenue from interest on loans and interest on bank deposits, gains and recoveries, as well as revenue from miscellaneous sources.

Contributions receivable

2.15 Contributions and contributions receivable are presented net of provision for estimated reductions in contribution revenue and doubtful accounts.

2.16 In-kind contributions of services that directly support approved operations and activities, and that have budgetary impact and can be reliably measured, are recognized and valued at fair value. Such contributions include the use of premises, vehicles and personnel.

2.17 Donated inventory or property, plant and equipment are valued at fair value and recognized as assets and revenue.

Accounts receivable

2.18 Receivables are recognized at their nominal value.

2.19 Provision for doubtful accounts is recognized when there is objective evidence that a receivable is impaired. In particular, a provision is recognized on the basis of historical collection experience. Impairment losses are recognized in the statement of financial performance.

Loans receivable and provision for loan losses

2.20.1   *Loans receivable*

Loans receivable represent loans from borrowers under the Agency's microfinance programme and microcredit community support programme, which offer targeted credit products through a revolving loan fund that serves its operations in all fields. Loans receivable are recognized at their outstanding principal balance.

2.20.2   *Provision for impairment of loans*

Each quarter, the Agency assesses whether a loan asset or group of loan assets is impaired. A group of loan assets is impaired and impairment losses are incurred only if there is objective evidence that there has been impairment as a result of one or more events ("loss events") occurring after the initial recognition of the asset and that the loss event or events have had an impact on the estimated future cash flows of the loan asset or group of loan assets that can be reliably estimated.

If, during the subsequent period, the amount of the estimated impairment loss increases or decreases because of an event occurring after the impairment was recognized, the previously recognized impairment loss is increased or reduced by adjusting the provision account.

2.20.3   *Related-party ("insider") loans*

The Agency provides credit facilities to staff, but not to the Executive Director of the Microfinance Department or to members of the Advisory Board. The loan conditions and interest rates for staff-clients are identical to those for other customers. Such loans are provided for consumption and housing.

2.20.4   *Accrued interest on loans*

Interest income on loans financed is accounted for on the accrual basis.

2.20.5   *Recoveries*

Any recoveries of previously written-off loans are reflected in the statement of financial performance for the period during which they are received.

Financial instruments

2.21 The Agency has applied the following IPSAS, which have been issued and are effective from 1 January 2013: IPSAS 28, Financial instruments: presentation; IPSAS 29, Financial instruments: recognition and measurement; and IPSAS 30, Financial instruments: disclosures. They establish the principles for recognizing and measuring financial assets and financial liabilities, for presenting financial instruments as liabilities or net assets/equity, for offsetting financial assets and financial liabilities, and requirements for disclosure.

2.22 Financial instruments are recognized when UNRWA becomes a party to the contractual provisions of the instrument until such time as the rights to receive cash flows from those assets have expired or have been transferred and UNRWA has transferred substantially all of the risks and rewards of ownership.

2.23 Loans, receivables and payables are non-derivative financial instruments with fixed or determinable payments that are not quoted in active markets. These financial instruments comprise contributions receivable in cash, loans receivable as part of the credit facilities of the Microfinance Department, other receivables and cash in bank accounts and accounts payable. All non-derivative financial instruments are recognized in the statement of financial position at their fair values. The nominal value of receivables and payables approximates the fair value of the transaction.

2.24 The Agency uses derivative financial instruments to hedge exchange risk. Foreign exchange forward contracts are revalued and the revaluation gain or loss is reported in the statement of financial performance if the contracts belong to the current year. For contracts relating to subsequent years, the revaluation gain or loss is reported in the statement of financial position. For revaluation at year-end, the market rate for the forward contract is obtained from the banks and these are compared against the forward rates to ascertain the gain or loss.

Financial risk management

2.25 The activities carried out by UNRWA expose it to various financial risks, primarily the effects of changes in foreign currency exchange rates. Consequently, the Agency's financial risk management policies are focused on the unpredictability of foreign exchange rates and are aimed at minimizing, where feasible, potential adverse effects on the financial performance of UNRWA. Financial risk management is carried out by a central treasury function using UNRWA technical guidelines covering such areas of financial risk as foreign exchange, the use of derivative financial instruments and the investment of excess liquidity.

Advances and prepayments

2.26 Advances and prepayments are recognized at their nominal value.

Inventories

2.27 Inventories are stated at the lower of cost or current replacement cost. The cost of inventories includes purchase cost, or fair value if donated in kind, and all other costs incurred in bringing the inventory into custody. Cost is determined using a weighted average cost formula.

2.28 Current replacement cost, which is used so that inventories can be distributed to beneficiaries at no or nominal charge, is the cost that the Agency would incur to acquire the asset on the reporting date.

2.29 Shelter work in progress is recognized as inventory and such inventories expensed in the period in which the shelter is handed over to the refugees.

2.30 A charge for impairment is recorded in the statement of financial performance for the year in which the inventory is determined to be impaired.

Property, plant and equipment

2.31 Property, plant and equipment items are stated at historical cost, less accumulated depreciation and any recognized impairment loss. For donated assets, fair value as at the date of acquisition is utilized as a proxy for historical cost. For property acquired before 1 January 2010, items were recognized at fair value as at that date and depreciated using the straight-line method over their estimated remaining useful lives.

2.32 Property, plant and equipment are capitalized in the financial statements if their cost exceeds a nominal value.

2.33 Subsequent costs are included in the asset's carrying amount or recognized as a separate asset, as appropriate, only when it is probable that future economic benefits or service potential associated with the item will flow to the Agency and the cost of the item can be measured reliably. All repairs and maintenance are charged to the statement of financial performance for the financial period during which they are incurred.

2.34 Depreciation is charged so as to allocate the cost of assets over their estimated useful lives using the straight-line method. The depreciation rates are as follows and are subject to annual review (property acquired before 2010 is not subject to the rates below):

(Percentage)

Asset type	Depreciation rate
Buildings and land improvements	
Buildings and land improvements	4
Prefabricated buildings	10
Short-life land improvements	14
Leasehold improvement	20
Vehicles	
Heavy trucks	5
Sedans, light buses and light trucks/or buses	10
Other vehicles	14
Equipment	
Long-life information and communications technology (ICT) equipment, medical equipment and technical vocational training equipment	14
General machinery and equipment, office equipment, medium-life ICT equipment and teaching and school equipment	20
Short-life ICT equipment, computers and printers	33
Microfinance Department office equipment	10
Furniture and fixtures	
Fixtures	14
Furniture	10-20

Capital work in progress

2.35 All capital expenses incurred on construction are accumulated in a separate account within property, plant and equipment. Upon the completion of construction, the accumulated cost is transferred to a property, plant and equipment account and depreciated on the basis of the aforementioned rates as at the date on which the completed asset is placed in service.

Intangible assets

2.36 Intangible assets are carried at historical cost, less accumulated amortization and any recognized impairment loss. For donated intangible assets, fair value as at the date of acquisition is used as a proxy for historical cost. Intangible assets are capitalized in the financial statements if their cost exceeds a nominal value.

2.37 Amortization is provided on a straight-line basis on all intangible assets of finite life, at rates that will allocate the cost or value of the assets to their estimated residual values. The estimated useful lives of classes of intangible assets are as follows and are subject to annual review:

Asset class	Useful life (years)
Software acquired externally	3
Software developed internally	6
Licences and rights	2
Copyrights	3

2.38 Intangible asset recognition requires the meeting of strict criteria with regard to being identifiable, being under the Agency's control and contributing future economic benefits or service potential that can be reliably measured. Remaining useful life is also a consideration. Expenditure on research activities, undertaken with the prospect of gaining new scientific or technical knowledge and understanding, is expensed as incurred.

Software acquisition and development

2.39 Acquired computer software licences are capitalized on the basis of costs incurred to acquire the specific software and bring it into use. Costs directly associated with the development of software for use by the Agency are capitalized as an intangible asset. Development activities include a plan or design for the production of new or substantially improved products and processes. Development expenditure is capitalized only if the development costs can be measured reliably, the product or process is technically and commercially feasible, future economic benefits are probable, and UNRWA intends to and has sufficient resources to complete development and to use the asset. The expenditure capitalized includes the costs of materials and direct labour and overhead costs that are directly attributable to preparing the asset for its intended use. Other development expenditure is recognized in the statement of financial performance as incurred: capitalized development expenditure is measured at cost, less accumulated amortization and accumulated impairment losses.

Impairment

2.40 Assets that are subject to depreciation or amortization are reviewed annually for impairment to ensure that the carrying amount is still considered to be recoverable. Impairment occurs through complete loss, major damage or obsolescence. In the case of a complete loss, full impairment is recorded. This impairment loss can be reversed in subsequent periods, subject to a maximum of the impairment loss recognized.

Operating leases

2.41 Leases where the lessor retains a significant portion of the risks and rewards inherent to ownership are classified as operating leases. Payments due under operating leases are charged to the statement of financial performance as an expense.

Payables and accruals

2.42 Payables and accruals represent present obligations of the Agency arising from past events.

Employee benefits

2.43 The Agency recognizes the following categories of employee benefits:

- Short-term employee benefits that fall due wholly within 12 months after the end of the accounting period during which employees render the related service;

- Post-employment benefits;

- Other long-term employee benefits;

- Termination benefits.

2.44 The Agency is a member organization participating in the United Nations Joint Staff Pension Fund, which was established by the General Assembly to provide retirement, death, disability and related benefits to employees. The Pension Fund is a funded, multi-employer defined benefit plan. As specified in article 3 (b) of the Regulations of the Fund, membership in the Fund shall be open to the specialized agencies and to any other international intergovernmental organization which participates in the common system of salaries, allowances and other conditions of service of the United Nations and the specialized agencies. All international staff members participate in the Fund.

2.45 The plan exposes participating organizations to actuarial risks associated with the current and former employees of other organizations participating in the United Nations Joint Staff Pension Fund, with the result that there is no consistent and reliable basis for allocating the obligation, plan assets and costs to individual organizations participating in the plan. Neither the Fund nor UNRWA, nor any other organization participating in the Fund, is in a position to identify its respective proportionate share of the defined benefit obligation, plan assets and costs associated with the plan with sufficient reliability for accounting purposes. Hence, UNRWA has treated this plan as if it were a defined contribution plan in accordance with the requirements set out in IPSAS 25, Employee benefits. The Agency's contributions to the plan during the financial period are recognized as expenses in the statement of financial performance.

2.46 All area staff members participate in the Area Staff Provident Fund, which is accounted for as a defined contribution retirement plan in accordance with IPSAS 25.

Provisions and contingent liabilities

2.47 Provisions are made for future liabilities and charges where UNRWA has a present legal or constructive obligation as a result of past events, it is probable that it will be required to settle the obligation, and the amount can be reasonably estimated.

2.48 Other material commitments, which do not meet the recognition criteria for liabilities, are disclosed in the notes to the financial statements as contingent liabilities when their existence will be confirmed only by the occurrence or non-occurrence of one or more uncertain future events not wholly within the control of UNRWA.

Interest revenue

2.49 Interest revenue is recognized over the period during which it is earned. The amount of interest on bank deposits is $0.344 million.

Programme support cost recovery

2.50 The Agency is entitled to a specific percentage of the expenditure incurred on certain projects according to agreements with donors. Programme support cost recoveries are recognized as income and represent recoveries of overhead costs incurred by the Agency to implement the related projects.

Fund accounting and segment reporting

2.51 A fund is a self-balancing accounting entity established to account for the transactions of a specified purpose or objective. Funds are segregated for the purpose of carrying out specific activities or attaining certain objectives in accordance with special regulations, restrictions or limitations. The financial statements are prepared on a fund accounting basis, showing at the end of the period the aggregated position of all UNRWA funds. Fund balances represent the accumulated residual of revenue and expenses.

2.52 A segment is a distinguishable activity or group of activities for which financial information is reported separately in order to evaluate an entity's past performance in achieving its objectives and for making decisions about the future allocation of resources. UNRWA classifies all projects, operations and fund activities into five segments:

- Unearmarked activities — comprising activities under the programme budget;
- Earmarked activities, which include:
  - Restricted activities: a series of recurring activities aimed at bringing about clearly specified objectives within a defined time period and a defined budget. This applies to activities related to both cash and in-kind contributions for the regular budget;
  - Emergency appeals: activities under an external funding request to respond to a rapid crisis or a protracted humanitarian crisis with emergency operations;
  - Projects: used to meet capital expenditure or development needs to improve or supplement existing programmes and systems;

- Microfinance: used to provide credit for enterprise activities, household consumption and housing needs that will improve the quality of life of householders and small-business owners and will help sustain jobs, reduce poverty, empower women and provide income-generating opportunities for Palestine refugees.

Budget comparison

2.53 The budget for the biennium 2014-2015 was submitted to the General Assembly. After consideration by the Assembly, the allocation and the appropriations were carried out by exercising the delegated authority.

2.54 The biennial budget is prepared on the modified cash basis and the statement of financial performance is prepared on the accrual basis. Owing to the different bases used for the preparation of budgets and financial statements, statement V, which provides a comparison of budget and actual amounts, is prepared on the same basis of accounting, classification and period as the approved budget, as required under IPSAS 24, Presentation of budget information in financial statements.

2.55 The comparison statement includes the original and final budget amounts, the actual amounts on the same basis as the corresponding budgetary amounts and an explanation of material differences between the budget and actual amounts.

2.56 Note 34 provides a reconciliation of actual amounts presented on the same basis as the budget with the actual amounts of net cash flows from operating activities, investing activities and financing activities presented in the financial statements, identifying separately any basis, timing and entity differences.

(f) Implementation of the new enterprise resource planning system

2.57 The Agency completed the implementation of the new SAP enterprise resource planning system (known as REACH) during 2015 and all balances were migrated from the legacy system. The new enterprise resource planning system replaces the previous financial, supply chain and human resource and payroll systems, resulting in changes in various areas including a new Chart of Accounts, changes in programme reporting structure, funding classification, project accounting, grant management, business warehouse reporting, business process and consolidation and other processes, thereby improving the efficiency of operations of the Agency.

Note 3
Amendments to the presentation of the 2014 financial statements

3.1 To reflect more accurately the value of inventory recorded in the books, the Agency recognized non-inventory items with the inventory maintained, especially as these items are stored in the agency warehouses until such time they are consumed by the owner departments. The accounting entries were effected in 2015; however, to achieve comparability, the presentation of the 2014 financial statement was amended to effect the below change of an increase in inventory and net equity by $10.8 million.

3.2 During the establishment of the new enterprise resource planning system, certain expenses were capitalized as software under development, pursuant to IPSAS standards, and included as part of intangible assets. Upon completion and final assessment, various expenses were deemed ineligible for capitalization as they relate to the maintenance rather than the enhancement of the related software. The costs were therefore de-capitalized and recorded in expenses. As the expenses were incurred during 2014 the presentation of comparatives was amended to reflect the decrease in intangible asset and net equity by $2.2 million. The impact of the amendments to the relevant balances is shown in the summary below:

(Thousands of United States dollars)

	2014 audited statement	Adjustment	2014 (amended)
Statement I: financial position			
Inventory	85 564	10 797	96 361
Intangible assets	33 346	(2 186)	31 160
Accumulated surplus/deficit	303 806	8 611	312 417
Statement III: changes in net assets/equity			
Accumulated surplus/deficit unearmarked opening balance	(83 384)	906	(82 478)
Accumulated surplus/deficit earmarked opening balance	387 190	(7 705)	394 895

Note 4
Cash and cash equivalents

4.1 Cash is held principally in United States dollar bank accounts. The composition of cash is as follows:

(Thousands of United States dollars)

	31 December 2015	31 December 2014
Cash in hand	7 370	17 446
Cash at banks	301 414	288 008
Total	**308 784**	**305 454**

4.2 The Agency held funds for other United Nations entities in the amount of $0.102 million as at 31 December 2015 and $1.557 million as at 31 December 2014.

4.3 The balances of cash and cash equivalents at banks as at 31 December 2015 were held in the currencies shown in the table below. Currency values have been converted at the United Nations official rates of exchange as at 1 January 2016.

Currency	Balance as at 31 December 2015			Balance as at 31 December 2014		
	Currency amount (thousands)	United Nations official rate of exchange	United States dollar amount (thousands)	Amount	United Nations official rate of exchange	United States dollar amount (thousands)
Australian dollar	0.61	1.37	0.445	0.02	1.228	0.016
Canadian dollar	150	1.385	108	173	1.163	149
Swiss franc	4 473	0.991	4 514	435	0.987	440
Danish krone	320	6.82	47	19 001	6.105	3 112
Egyptian pound	194	7.83	25	91	7.153	13
Euro	26 556	0.914	29 055	8 198	0.82	9 998
Pound sterling	10 480	0.675	15 526	714	0.644	1 109
Jordanian dinar	19 712	0.708	27 842	3 749	0.708	5 296
Yen	1 104	120.45	9	632 953	120.67	5 245
Lebanese pound	4 863 805	1 513.5	3 214	4 181 617	1 513	2 764
New Israeli sheqel	12 299	3.883	3 167	12 687	3.913	3 242
Norwegian krone	389	8.688	45	846	7.437	114
Swedish krona	320 657	8.369	38 315	595	7.852	76
Syrian pound	15 897	338	47	63 414	196.04	323
United States dollar	179 501	1	179 501	256 128	1	256 128
Total			**301 414**			**288 008**

Note 5
Loans receivable

5.1   Loans receivable include loans outstanding from funds disbursed from the Microfinance Department and the microcredit community support programme both through an initial donor contribution (first-time loans) and from revolving loan funds. The Microfinance Department operates as a separate department within UNRWA. The microcredit community support programme is a subprogramme of the Social Services Division of the Relief and Social Services Department of UNRWA.

5.2   The composition of loans receivable, net of provision for bad debts by maturity, is as follows:

(Thousands of United States dollars)

	31 December 2015			31 December 2014		
	Microfinance Department	Microcredit community support programme	Total	Microfinance Department	Microcredit community support programme	Total
Current	21 352	1 333	22 685	19 820	1 358	21 178
Non-current	2 471	937	3 408	1 547	1 047	2 594
Total	**23 823**	**2 270**	**26 093**	**21 367**	**2 405**	**23 772**

Provision for loans receivable

5.3   The change in the provision for doubtful loans receivable is as follows:

(Thousands of United States dollars)

	2015			2014		
	Microfinance Department	*Microcredit community support programme*	*Total*	*Microfinance Department*	*Microcredit community support programme*	*Total*
Beginning balance as at	(1 527)	(73)	**(1 600)**	(1 339)	(20)	**(1 359)**
Additions	(702)	(2)	**(704)**	(1 048)	(53)	**(1 101)**
Less: write-off	810	77	**887**	860	–	**860**
Ending balance	**(1 419)**	**2**	**(1 417)**	**(1 527)**	**(73)**	**(1 600)**

Provision for loan losses

5.4   For the microcredit community support programme, the provision for doubtful loans is equal to 3 per cent of the outstanding amount of the loan portfolio, excluding loans to UNRWA staff, for which no provision is made.

5.5   For the Microfinance Department, the provision for doubtful loans is based on an "aged portfolio at-risk report", which is applied to the total amount outstanding of each loan. On the basis of empirical experience, historical record and market knowledge, it was determined that the following general provision is required for delinquent and defaulting Microfinance Department loans:

Loan status	*Provision*
Current	1% general provision
1-30 days overdue	5% general provision
31-60 days overdue	10% general provision
61-90 days overdue	25% general provision
91-120 days overdue	50% general provision
121-180 days overdue	75% general provision
181-360 days overdue	100% general provision

5.6   Effective September 2012, a special impairment on outstanding Microfinance Department loans was adopted in the Syrian Arab Republic to mitigate the risk posed by the situation of armed conflict. The rates of reserve calculation are set out below for the special impairment at year-end 2014 and 2015:

Loan status	Provision
1-30 days overdue	95% special impairment
31-60 days overdue	90% special impairment
61-90 days overdue	75% special impairment
91-120 days overdue	50% special impairment
121-180 days overdue	25% special impairment
181-360 days overdue	0% special impairment

5.7 Based upon the above percentages, if a loan is not serviced, an increasing reserve should be provided for. This provision will be shown in the statement of financial performance for the period. On a monthly basis, an adjustment is made to reflect the changes in the general provision. When a loan is in arrears for 360 days or more, there exists objective evidence of an impairment loss and the loan has been fully provisioned in the general provision, it will be written off. Criteria used to determine that there is objective evidence of an impairment loss may include: indications that the borrower or a group of borrowers is experiencing significant financial difficulty; default or delinquency in payments of interest or principal; breach of loan covenants or conditions; deterioration in the value of collateral; the probability exists that they will enter bankruptcy or other financial reorganization; and observable data indicate that there is a measurable decrease in the estimated future cash flows, such as changes in arrears or economic conditions that correlate with defaults. Recovery of written-off loans will continue to be pursued through the collection and compliance section of the Department.

Note 6
Contributions receivable

6.1 Contributions receivable represents confirmed and binding pledges outstanding from donors that are due within 12 months. The following is a breakdown of contributions receivable balances by donor category at the end of the year:

(Thousands of United States dollars)

	31 December 2015	31 December 2014
Due from Governments	27 866	25 631
Due from intergovernmental organizations	10 308	11 318
Due from non-governmental organizations	4 552	1 030
Due from United Nations organizations	2 046	1 240
Provision against contributions receivable	(5 133)	(1 031)
Total contributions receivable	**39 639**	**38 188**

6.2 There are no non-current receivables due after 12 months from 31 December 2015.

6.3 Contributions receivable relate to donor contributions for each of the five identified segments. Donor contributions may include restrictions that require

UNRWA to use the contribution for a specific project, activity or country within a specified time period.

6.4   Contributions receivable are shown net of provision for estimated reductions in contribution revenue and doubtful accounts.

6.5   The change in the provision for doubtful contributions receivable is as follows:

(Thousands of United States dollars)

	31 December 2015	31 December 2014
Beginning balance	(1 031)	(550)
Reduction in provision/adjustment	3	310
Addition during the period	(4 275)	(791)
Less: write-offs	170	–
Ending balance	**(5 133)**	**(1 031)**

6.6   The provision for doubtful contributions receivable is estimated at the following percentages of outstanding contributions receivable:

(Percentage)

Governments	Less than 2 years	0
	From 2 years to less than 3 years	50
	3 years or more	100

6.7   After six years, the doubtful debt and the write-off request, together with the supporting documents, should be submitted to the Director of Finance for approval after all collection efforts have been exhausted. The Commissioner-General has delegated his authority to write off amounts less than $1 million to the Director of Finance. Uncollectible amounts of $1 million or greater must be approved by the Commissioner-General in order to be written off.

Note 7
Accounts receivable

7.1   Accounts receivable are due to be collected within 12 months and comprise the following:

(Thousands of United States dollars)

	Relevant note	31 December 2015	31 December 2014
Value-added tax receivable	7.1.1	104 607	100 177
Other accounts receivable	7.1.2	12 548	7 453
Less provisions	7.1.3	(83 386)	(65 023)
Accounts receivable net of provisions		**33 769**	**42 607**

Value-added tax receivable

7.1.1 Value-added tax receivable represents amounts receivable from Governments for value-added tax paid by the Agency that is subject to reimbursement. The composition of value-added tax receivable by government is as follows:

(Thousands of United States dollars)

	31 December 2015	31 December 2014
Value-added tax receivable from the Palestinian Authority	100 594	96 822
Value-added tax receivable from the Government of Israel	3 467	1 582
Value-added tax receivable from the Government of Lebanon	546	1 773
Total	**104 607**	**100 177**

Other accounts receivable

7.1.2 Other accounts receivable comprise the following:

(Thousands of United States dollars)

	31 December 2015	31 December 2014
Miscellaneous receivable	6 909	3 435
Personal accounts of staff members	3 166	3 830
Refundable utility deposits	125	188
Due from Area Staff Provident Fund[a]	2 348	–
Total	**12 548**	**7 453**

[a] See note 14A.1.

7.1.3 *Provisions and write-offs*

(Thousands of United States dollars)

	31 December 2015				31 December 2014		
	Value-added tax	*Accounts receivable*	*Microfinance Department*	*Total*	*Value-added tax*	*Accounts receivable*	*Total*
Beginning balance	(64 163)	(803)	(57)	**(65 023)**	(46 686)	(1 008)	**(47 694)**
Additions	(18 327)	(37)	–	**(18 364)**	(17 534)	59	**(17 475)**
Less: write-offs	–	1	–	**1**	–	146	**146**
Ending balance	**(82 490)**	**(839)**	**(57)**	**(83 386)**	**(64 220)**	**(803)**	**(65 023)**

7.2 The provisions for value-added tax receivable and accounts receivable are estimated amounts based on the aged analysis of the outstanding amounts as at the reporting date. These provisions have been calculated on the basis of past experience and the likelihood of collecting the outstanding amounts over the specific periods, as shown below.

(Percentage)

Value-added tax receivable	Less than 2 years	0
	From 2 years to less than 3 years	50
	3 years or more	100
Other receivable	1 year or more	100

7.3   After six years for value-added tax receivable and three years for other receivables, the doubtful debt and the write-off request, together with the supporting documents, may be submitted to the Director of Finance for approval after all collection efforts have been exhausted. In some instances, collection efforts continue after the time periods specified above have elapsed.

7.4   The 2015 additions for accounts receivable (provisions, see note 7.1.3) reflect a net increase of $14.301 million.

Note 8
Other assets

8.1   Included in other assets are prepaid expenses and advances to suppliers. Prepaid expenses and advances to suppliers totalled $4.246 million as at 31 December 2015 and $7.475 million as at 31 December 2014. Included therein are prepayments to staff in the amount of $0.269 million as at 31 December 2015 and $0.159 million as at 31 December 2014.

8.2   The composition of prepaid expenses and advances to suppliers as at 31 December 2015 is shown below. The full amount of non-current assets represents advances to suppliers.

(Thousands of United States dollars)

	31 December 2015	*31 December 2014*
Current		
Advances to supplier	3 789	7 082
Prepayment to staff	269	159
Non-current		
Advances to supplier	188	234
Total	**4 246**	**7 475**

Note 9
Inventories

9.1   Inventories consist of the following:

(Thousands of United States dollars)

Type	31 December 2015	31 December 2014 (restated)
Warehouse	45 015	42 677
Pharmacy/clinic	17 565	7 238
In transit	4 410	3 680
Production unit	162	269
Shelter under construction	23 293	34 916
Non-Agency installations	11 463	7 581
Total	**101 908**	**96 361**

9.2   Warehouse inventory comprises four main categories of items that are distributed to refugees or used to provide services to refugees: medical supplies, general supplies, food and motor transport. During the year, as part of the transition to the new enterprise resource planning system, non-inventory items were reclassified as inventory items to enhance the visibility of all items bought by quantity and value, strengthen accountability, track spending and use this for strategic sourcing analysis, with an integrated application to manage inventory accurately across multiple warehouses and locations.

9.3   Inventory in transit are materials for which significant risks and rewards are transferred to UNRWA and are yet to be received at the warehouse. With the introduction of the new enterprise resource planning system, such goods are tracked and recorded in the virtual warehouses. The goods which are received and recorded in the virtual warehouses are recorded as inventories. Materials for which goods receipt notes were not recorded are shown as inventory in transit.

9.4   Pharmacy/clinic inventory represents medical supplies distributed from the warehouse and held in the respective pharmacies and clinics for the five fields.

9.5   Production unit inventory relates to the Agency's self-supporting production unit, which is the embroidery centre located in the Gaza Strip. This unit is governed by separate instructions for effective management control and performance assessment. Inventories of the production unit are reported at cost, under assets in the financial statements.

9.6   The components of the production unit inventory are as follows:

(Thousands of United States dollars)

	31 December 2015	31 December 2014
Raw materials inventory — embroidery	67	70
Work in progress — embroidery	2	2
Finished goods — embroidery	93	197
Total	**162**	**269**

9.7   Impairment expense for inventory in the amount of $0.025 million was recorded in 2015 ($0.456 million in 2014).

9.8   In accordance with IPSAS 12, inventory has been adjusted to reflect the net realizable value based on current replacement cost. An amount of $2.639 million has been included in the cost of supplies and consumables and disclosed in note 28 accordingly. No such adjustment was necessary in 2014 as the carrying value was lower than replacement cost.

Note 10
Derivative financial instruments

Nature of financial instruments

10.1 Details of the significant accounting policies and methods adopted, including the criteria for recognition and derecognition, the basis of measurement and the basis on which gains and losses are recognized in respect of each class of financial asset and financial liability, are set out in note 2.

10.2 The financial instruments of UNRWA comprise contributions receivable in cash, loans receivable as part of the Microfinance Department credit facilities, other receivables, cash in bank accounts, financial derivative forward contracts and accounts payable.

Financial derivatives

10.3.1 All the outstanding financial derivative forward contracts were revalued as at 31 December 2015; the impact on financial position and on financial performance is summarized below.

(Thousands of United States dollars)

	31 December 2015	31 December 2014
Realized gain	17 925	7 698
Realized (loss)	(6 521)	(3 799)
Total realized gain	**11 404**	**3 899**
Unrealized gain/asset	7 658	4 877
Unrealized loss/(liability)	(1 085)	(6 755)

10.3.2 All outstanding contracts as at 31 December 2014 were matured during financial year 2015. UNRWA entered into several forward contracts during 2015, some of which matured in the same year, resulting in a net realized gain of $11.404 million, classified as financial derivatives gain under other revenues in the statement of financial performance.

10.3.3 The Agency entered into various forward contracts in 2015. The outstanding contracts as at 31 December 2015 are revalued using the market rate. Contracts which resulted in revaluation loss of $1.085 million are disclosed as derivative financial liabilities in the statement of financial position.

10.3.4 Revaluation of outstanding contracts resulted in a revaluation gain of $7.658 million. The result is disclosed as derivative financial assets under current assets in the statement of financial position.

Credit risk

10.4 The Agency has limited credit risk because its donors are generally of a high credit standing. Contributions receivable comprise primarily amounts due from sovereign nations. Details of contributions receivable, including provision for reductions in contribution revenue, are provided in note 6.

10.5 The greatest area of credit risk arises from loans provided by the Microfinance Department. The Department manages credit risk by:

- Establishing ceilings on amounts of direct credit for each product linked to the cash flow of each client;

- Providing a range of products to different sectors and segments to spread credit and reduce concentration;

- Formulating credit policies by product covering collateral requirements and credit compliance with regulatory requirements in each jurisdiction;

- Establishing the authorization structure for the approval and renewal of credit facilities;

- Reviewing and assessing credit risk in excess of designated limits prior to facilities being committed to customers. Renewals of facilities are subject to the same process;

- Developing and maintaining a risk-grading system in order to categorize exposure according to when impairment provisions are required against specific credit exposures;

- Providing guidance and training to improve skills of staff in order to promote best practice in the management of credit risk.

10.6 In 2015, the credit risk in the Syrian Arab Republic and the Gaza Strip continued to increase as a result of conflict. The Microfinance Department manages this risk by increasing provisions as the portfolio at risk increases as a percentage of the full portfolio.

10.7 The Agency has its cash deposited with various banks and is therefore exposed to the risk that a bank will default in its obligation towards it. However, UNRWA holds all significant cash deposits in international banks with a high credit rating.

10.8 There is no perceived risk that other receivables may not be liquidated when they fall due.

Interest rate risk

10.9 The Agency deposits its funds in short-term fixed interest accounts and therefore has no significant interest rate risk exposure.

Foreign currency risk

10.10 The Agency receives contributions from donors in currencies other than the primary currency of the expenditures, United States dollars. In 2015, 42 per cent of contributions to the programme budget were denominated in the United States dollar base currency and 58 per cent were denominated in other currencies. The Microfinance Department lends in different currencies, according to the Agency's fields of operation, with the United States dollar used in the Gaza Strip, the Jordanian dinar used in Jordan and the West Bank, and the Syrian pound used in the Syrian Arab Republic.

10.11 Furthermore, some field office expenditures are incurred in non-United States dollar currencies. The Agency is therefore exposed to foreign currency exchange risk arising from fluctuations of currency exchange rates. Foreign exchange forward contracts are used to hedge the non-United States dollar exchange exposure for donor contributions.

10.12 To protect its assets and cash flow against adverse currency movements, UNRWA adopts a conservative risk management approach, hedging to minimize its exposure to exchange rate fluctuations. In order to hedge the currency risk, UNRWA enters into forward contracts to remove the risk of an appreciation of the United States dollar and to provide a known, fixed income amount. UNRWA also enters into forward contracts to hedge the risk of fluctuation in currency adjustment factor expense for area staff in the West Bank and the Gaza Strip.

10.13 As at 31 December 2015, 60 per cent of cash held in banks was denominated in the United States dollar base currency, 12 per cent was denominated in local currencies used by UNRWA field offices to support operating activities, and the remaining cash at banks was held in other currencies. A full breakdown of cash held at banks in currencies other than the United States dollar is provided in note 4.

Note 11
Property, plant and equipment

11.1.1 The table below presents a summary of property, plant and equipment as at 31 December 2015.

(Thousands of United States dollars)

Description	Land	Buildings	Leasehold improvements	Furniture and fittings	Office and computer equipment	Motor vehicles	Construction in progress	Assets not placed in service	Total (2015)	Total (2014)
Cost										
As at 1 January	16 250	461 432	583	397	36 501	36 238	26 964	3 086	581 451	553 580
+ Additions in year	–	21 620	–	93	3 747	6 167	14 347	(2 631)	43 343	32 605
(-) Disposals/adjustment in year[a]	–	5 353	–	–	321	613	–	–	6 287	2 989
Balance as at 31 December (A)	**16 250**	**477 699**	**583**	**490**	**39 927**	**41 793**	**41 311**	**455**	**618 508**	**583 195**
Depreciation										
Balance as at 1 January	–	81 025	429	280	25 654	20 740	–	–	128 128	112 366
+ Depreciation in year	–	17 539	95	44	4 151	3 336	–	–	25 164	24 507
(-) Depreciation on disposals/adjustments in year[a]	–	1 820	–	–	304	604	–	–	2 728	1 573
Balance as at 31 December (B)		**96 744**	**524**	**324**	**29 501**	**23 472**	**–**	**–**	**150 565**	**135 299**
Impairment										
Balance as at 1 January	–	3 252	–	–	1	85	–	–	3 338	–
+ Impairment in year	–	104	–	–	–	–	–	–	104	–
(-) Impairment reversed and on disposal in year	–	277	–	–	–	–	–	–	277	–
Balance as at 31 December (C)	**–**	**3 079**	**–**	**–**	**1**	**85**	**–**	**–**	**3 165**	**(2 089)**
Net book value as at 31 December (A)-(B)-(C)	**16 250**	**377 876**	**59**	**166**	**10 426**	**18 236**	**41 311**	**455**	**464 778**	**449 985**

[a] See note 11.1.2.

11.1.2 Net cost of disposal is $3.264 million, which comprises the following:

(Thousands of United States dollars)

	2015	*2014*
Original cost of disposal	6 287	2 989
Accumulated depreciation	(2 728)	(1 573)
Accumulated impairment	(295)	–
Cost of disposal as per note 11.1.1	**3 264**	**1 416**

The proceeds from the sale of assets and the gain and loss on the class of assets is as below:

(Thousands of United States dollars)

	2015	*2014*
Loss on disposal	3 261	1 348
Gain on disposal	(5)	(81)
Proceeds from sale of assets	8	150
Net disposal/adjustments as per note 11.1.1	**3 264**	**1 416**

11.1.3 On transition from the legacy system to the new enterprise resource planning system and as part of data cleansing, the classification of assets, life of the assets and accumulated depreciation were reviewed and adjusted accordingly. The net value of the net assets as at 31 December 2015 is shown below:

(Thousands of United States dollars)

	Original cost	*Accumulated depreciation*	*Accumulated impairment*	*Net cost*
Balance as at 31 December 2014	583 195	(133 210)	–	449 985
Change as per data cleansing	(1 744)	5 082	(3 338)	–
Balance as at 1 January 2015	**581 451**	**(128 128)**	**(3 338)**	**449 985**

11.2 In addition to the active assets valued at $464.778 million, the Agency continues to utilize fully depreciated assets with a gross carrying value of $37.024 million.

Note 12
Intangible assets

12.1 Intangible assets are summarized as follows:

(Thousands of United States dollars)

Description	Software acquired separately	Software developed internally	Licenses and rights	Copyrights	Work in progress	Total	Restated 2014 Total
					2015		
Cost							
As at 1 January	542	–	–	–	30 694	31 236	17 342
+ Additions in 2015	2 534	38 185	–	–	(30 192)	10 527	14 068
(-)/+ Disposals and adjustments in year	9	–	–	–	–	9	(173)
Revaluation in year	–	–	–	–	–	–	–
Balance as at 31 December (A)	**3 076**	**38 185**	**–**	**–**	**502**	**41 772**	**31 236**
Amortization and impairment							
Balance as at 1 January	76	–	–	–	–	76	5
Amortization in year	679	4 481	–	–	–	5 160	132
(-)/+ Amortization on disposals and adjustments in year	9	–	–	–	–	9	(61)
Impairment in year	–	–	–	–	–	–	–
(-) Impairment reversed in year	–	–	–	–	–	–	–
Balance as at 31 December (B)	**755**	**4 481**	**–**	**–**	**–**	**5 245**	**76**
Net book value as at 31 December (A)-(B)	**2 320**	**33 704**	**–**	**–**	**502**	**36 526**	**31 160**

12.2   In 2015, the Agency completed development of the new enterprise resource planning system, and the relevant internally developed software, amounting to $38.2 million dollars, has been included in intangible assets shown in the table above accordingly.

**Note 13
Accounts payable and accruals**

13.1   Accounts payable consist of the following:

(Thousands of United States dollars)

	Reference	31 December 2015	31 December 2014
Supplier accounts payable	Note 13.1.1	26 480	36 309
Accrued expenses	Note 13.1.2	33 514	32 723
Other accounts payable	Note 13.1.3	7 299	13 524
Accounts payable, non-current	Note 13.1.4	9 875	9 875
Due to Area Staff Provident Fund	Note 14A.1	–	3 995
Total		**77 168**	**96 426**

The composition of accounts payable is as follows:

(Thousands of United States dollars)

	31 December 2015	31 December 2014
Current	67 293	86 551
Non-current	9 875	9 875
Total	**77 168**	**96 426**

Supplier accounts payable

13.1.1 Supplier accounts payable represent outstanding amounts payable to vendors for goods and services received.

Accrued expenses

13.1.2 Accrued expenses include the following:

(Thousands of United States dollars)

	31 December 2015	31 December 2014
Accrued expenses for services and utilities	26 587	26 163
Area staff group medical insurance	1 007	1 877
Accrued salaries, wages and other expenses	121	930
Other salary-related payable	3 665	3 615
Payable — reclassifications of accounts receivable balance staff	2 134	138
Total	**33 514**	**32 723**

Other accounts payable

13.1.3 Other accounts payable consist of the following:

(Thousands of United States dollars)

	31 December 2015	31 December 2014
Deposits received	172	186
West Bank water supply, Palestinian Authority	173	104
Unpaid cheques	–	3
Funds held for other United Nations entities	101	1 557
Interest payable for projects	1 212	1 370
Miscellaneous accounts payable	1 032	3 495
Accounts payable — goods in transit	–	4 850
Staff liabilities payable	2 466	1 738
Unearned income canteen rent	2 143	221
Total	**7 299**	**13 524**

Accounts payable, non-current

13.1.4 Accounts payable, non-current, consist of the following:

(Thousands of United States dollars)

	31 December 2015	*31 December 2014*
OPEC Fund for International Development PalFund Trust Fund — Microfinance Department	9 875	9 875
Total	**9 875**	**9 875**

Note 14
Employee pension fund

14A
UNRWA Area Staff Provident Fund

14A.1 The UNRWA Area Staff Provident Fund established under article XIII of the Agency's Financial Regulations, is a retirement benefit plan that applies to all area staff members and vests after six months of service. UNRWA has treated this plan as if it were a defined contribution plan in accordance with the requirements of IPSAS 25. The Agency's contributions to the plan during the financial period are recognized as expenses in the statement of financial performance. The balances outstanding with the Provident Fund as at 31 December 2015 and as at 31 December 2014 are shown below.

(Thousands of United States dollars)

	31 December 2015	*31 December 2014*
Opening balance	3 995	10 576
Employee contributions	48 487	48 265
Agency contributions	55 611	54 087
Withdrawals	(44 808)	(51 609)
Area Staff Provident Fund employee loans	(31 833)	(23 874)
Area Staff Provident Fund loan commission	129	107
Current account with Provident Fund	(33 929)	(33 557)
Total	**(2 348)**	**3 995**

14B
United Nations Joint Staff Pension Fund: international staff

14B.1 The Regulations of the United Nations Joint Staff Pension Fund state that the Pension Board shall have an actuarial valuation made of the Fund at least once every three years by the consulting actuary. The practice of the Pension Board has been to carry out an actuarial valuation every two years using the open group aggregate method. The primary purpose of the actuarial valuation is to determine whether the current and estimated future assets of the Pension Fund will be sufficient to meet its liabilities.

14B.2 The Agency's financial obligation to the Pension Fund consists of its mandated contribution at the rate established by the General Assembly (currently 7.9 per cent for participants and 15.8 per cent for member organizations), together with any share of any actuarial deficiency payments under article 26 of the Regulations of the Pension Fund. Such deficiency payments are payable only if and when the General Assembly invokes the provisions of article 26, following a determination that there is a requirement for deficiency payments based on an assessment of the actuarial sufficiency of the Pension Fund as at the valuation date. Each member organization shall contribute towards this deficiency an amount proportionate to the total contributions that each paid during the three years preceding the valuation date.

14B.3 The actuarial valuation performed as at 31 December 2013 revealed an actuarial deficit of 0.72 per cent (1.87 per cent in the 2011 valuation) of pensionable remuneration, implying that the theoretical contribution rate required to achieve balance as at 31 December 2013 was 24.42 per cent of pensionable remuneration, compared to the actual contribution rate of 23.7 per cent. The next actuarial valuation will be conducted as at 31 December 2015. The results of the valuation are expected later in the year.

14B.4 As at 31 December 2013, the funded ratio of actuarial assets to actuarial liabilities, assuming no future pension adjustments, was 127.5 per cent (130.0 per cent in the 2011 valuation). The funded ratio was 91.2 per cent (86.2 per cent in the 2011 valuation) when the current system of pension adjustments was taken into account.

14B.5 After assessing the actuarial sufficiency of the Fund, the consulting actuary concluded that, as at 31 December 2013, there was no requirement for deficiency payments under article 26 of the Regulations of the Fund given that the actuarial value of assets exceeded the actuarial value of all accrued liabilities under the Fund. In addition, the market value of assets also exceeded the actuarial value of all accrued liabilities as at the valuation date. At the time of reporting, the General Assembly had not invoked the provisions of article 26.

14B.6 In December 2012 and April 2013, respectively, the General Assembly authorized, for new participants in the Fund, an increase in the normal retirement age and the mandatory age of separation to 65 years, effective from 1 January 2014. The related change to the Pension Fund's Regulations was approved by the Assembly in December 2013. The increase in the normal retirement age is reflected in the actuarial valuation of the Fund as at 31 December 2013.

14B.7 During 2015, the Agency's paid contributions to the Pension Fund amounted to $8.160 million (compared with $8.232 million in 2014). Contributions due in 2016 are expected to amount to $8.32 million.

14B.8 The Board of Auditors carries out an annual audit of the Pension Fund and reports to the Pension Board on the audit every year. The Pension Fund publishes quarterly reports on its investments, which can be viewed by visiting the Fund's website (www.unjspf.org).

Note 15
Staff end-of-service and termination benefits

15.1   The Agency recognizes the following categories of employee benefits:

- Short-term employee benefits due to be settled within 12 months after the end of the accounting period during which employees render the related service;

- Post-employment benefits;

- Other long-term employee benefits;

- Termination benefits.

(Thousands of United States dollars)

	31 December 2015	31 December 2014
Current	77 350	65 481
Non-current	620 087	494 786
Total	**697 436**	**560 267**

(Thousands of United States dollars)

	31 December 2015	31 December 2014
Annual leave encashment for area staff	43 617	32 869
End-of-service liability for area staff	650 035	524 540
Short-term employee benefits for international staff not funded through the United Nations regular budget	2 649	2 371
Long-term employee benefits for international staff not funded through the United Nations regular budget	1 135	488
Total	**697 436**	**560 268**

Short-term employee benefits for area staff

15.2   Short-term employee benefits consist of the annual leave of area staff. The amount of liability is calculated on the basis of the accumulated leave balances in the human resources module as at 31 December 2015. The total employee annual leave liability as at 31 December 2015 amounted to $43.617 million (compared with $32.869 million at 31 December 2014).

End-of-service liabilities for area staff

15.3   Area staff end-of-service and termination benefit liabilities are determined by professional actuaries or calculated by UNRWA on the basis of personnel data and past payment experience. As at 31 December 2015, total employee benefits liabilities amounted to $650.035 million (compared with $524.540 million as at 31 December 2014). The end-of-service benefits are fully unfunded. However, UNRWA allocates funding each year equivalent to the cash payout for that particular year.

15.4   In accordance with the requirements set out in IPSAS 25, the actuary has used the projected unit credit actuarial method to assess the plan's liabilities. Under this method a "projected accrued benefit" is calculated for each benefit that will accrue for all active members of the plan. The projected accrued benefit is based on the plan's accrual formula and on the service period as at the valuation date but using a member's final compensation projected to the age at which it is assumed that the employee will leave active service. The plan liability is the actuarial present value of the projected accrued benefits as at the valuation date for all active employees.

Normal and early retirement benefit

15.5   In the case of normal and early retirement, area staff are paid end-of-service benefits in accordance with rule 109.2 of the UNRWA Area Staff Rules. The criteria and assumptions used in calculating normal and early retirement benefits according to the actuarial method under IPSAS include the following: (a) all area staff employees are eligible, and the normal retirement age is considered to be from 60 to 62 years, plus a minimum service period of three years; (b) at the age of 60, the staff member has the option to extend his or her retirement age to 62; in this context, it is assumed that 25 per cent of the staff opt for immediate retirement upon attaining the age of 60; (c) the amount payable is calculated on the basis of the formula of base salary times 11 per cent times number of completed years of service before 1 January 2015 plus base salary times 12 per cent times number of completed years of service after 1 January 2015; (d) the service period is prorated until the last completed month of service; and (e) the base salary is the basic matrix salary without allowances. However, in Jordan, Lebanon and the Syrian Arab Republic, the basic matrix salary is adjusted for the fluctuation of the local currency against the United States dollar. In the West Bank, the basic matrix salary is adjusted for the fluctuation of the Jordanian dinar against the United States dollar.

15.6   The benefit referred to above is also payable in the case of early voluntary retirement. The conditions for early voluntary retirement are as follows: (a) attainment of the age of 50 to 59, with 10 years of service or more; (b) a service period of 25 years or more; (c) attainment of the age of 45 to 49, with a service period of 10 years or more; and (d) 20 to 24 years of service. The aforementioned eligibility criteria for early retirement are listed in descending order and are subject to an annual budget set by the Agency.

Termination in the interests of the Agency

15.7   Area staff are paid end-of-service benefits in accordance with rule 109.9 of the UNRWA Area Staff Rules if the termination is as stipulated in rule 109.1 of the Staff Rules and is in the interests of the Agency as reflected in the following criteria: (a) the service period must be equal to or greater than one year; (b) the employee is paid under either of the following two schemes, with the benefit amount and the application terms varying by years of qualified service and attained age:

Years of qualifying service	Months of base salary
0	0
1	1
2	1
3	2
4	3
5	4
6	5
7	6
8	7
9 or more	8

Age	Months of base salary
46	8.25
47	8.50
48	8.75
49	9.00
50	9.25
51	9.50
52	9.75
53	10.00
54	10.25
55	10.50

(c) the benefit is not paid if separation from service is initiated by the employee (e.g. through resignation); (d) the service period is prorated until the last completed month of service; and (e) the base salary is the basic matrix salary without allowances. However, in Jordan and Lebanon, the basic matrix salary is adjusted for the fluctuation of the local currency against the United States dollar. In the West Bank, the basic matrix salary is adjusted for the fluctuation of the Jordanian dinar against the United States dollar.

Death benefits

15.8   Death benefits for area staff are paid in accordance with rule 109.8 of the UNRWA Area Staff Rules. In the event of separation as a result of the death of an area staff member, the Agency shall pay a death benefit to the staff member's nominated beneficiary or beneficiaries. The death benefit shall be computed either: (a) as 11 per cent of the deceased staff member's ending annual salary and cost-of-living allowance (positive or negative) for each year of qualifying service before 1 January 2015 and 12 per cent for each year of qualifying service after 1 January 2015, plus a supplemental benefit representing 50 per cent of ending annual salary and cost-of-living allowance (positive or negative); or (b) as 200 per cent of ending annual salary and cost-of-living allowance (positive or negative), whichever is greater.

Disability benefits

15.9   Area staff are paid in accordance with UNRWA Area Staff Rule 109.7 if terminated on the stated ground that they are, for reasons of health, incapacitated insofar as further service with the Agency. In the event of the disability of a staff member on or after 1 September 1987 and subject to paragraphs 3 to 6 of the above-mentioned rule, a disability benefit is computed either: (a) as 11 per cent of ending annual salary and cost-of-living allowance (positive or negative) for each year of qualifying service before 1 January 2015 and 12 per cent for each year of qualifying service after 1 January 2015; or (b) as 200 per cent of ending annual salary and cost-of-living allowance (positive or negative), whichever is greater.

Reconciliation of end-of-service benefits

15.10 The interest costs and service costs incurred during the year have been directly accounted for in the statement of financial performance. The amount of interest costs, service costs and past service costs accounted for is shown in the table below.

15.11 IPSAS 25 allows the actuarial gains and losses that are within the corridor to be recognized outside the statement of financial performance and requires the presentation of the actuarial gains and losses in the statement of changes in net assets/equity. The amount of actuarial (losses) presented in the statement of changes in net assets/equity is $20.170 million (which includes the discount rate change during the year).

15.12 Interest costs and service costs amounted to $68.944 million as at 31 December 2015 (compared with $57.973 million for 2014). The actuarial (gains) losses are directly accounted for in the statement of changes in net assets/equity in accordance with IPSAS 25. In the 2015 valuation of end-of-service liabilities, the actuaries determined actuarial gains to be $8.841 million (excluding the discount rate change during the year). Accordingly, in the cash flow statement the actuarial gains were added rather than deducted because they were directly accounted for in the statement of changes in net assets/equity.

15.13 Effective 1 January 2015, the following enhancements/changes were introduced to the end-of-service benefit for local staff:

(a)   Inclusion of the currency adjustment factor in the end-of-service benefit: the Agency pays employees in Gaza and the West Bank a currency adjustment factor, which compensates employees for the depreciation of United States dollars against the Israeli sheqel. However, the currency adjustment factor as a pay element was not part of the qualifying salary used for the calculations of the end-of-service benefit. Effective 1 January 2015, the Agency will gradually include the adjustment for Gaza and the West Bank in the basic salary that qualifies for the end-of-service benefit. The inclusion of the currency adjustment factor will be done gradually every six months, from 1 January 2015 to 1 January 2017, by applying an increase of approximately 3 per cent, which will have an impact on the total increase in salaries by around 14.5 per cent (other things being equal) for Gaza and West Bank fields.

(b)   12 per cent of the base salary for each service year after 1 January 2015: the Agency will pay an end-of-service benefit of 12 per cent for each year of service after 1 January 2015 and 11 per cent for each year of service before 1 January 2015.

15.14 Given the benefit structure and assumptions used in the valuation of the end-of-service benefit, the benefit enhancements outlined above increased the present value of the defined benefit obligation. Under IPSAS 25, any change in the benefit terms that results in a change in the present value of the defined benefit obligation gives rise to a past service cost, which could be positive or negative. The past service costs resulting from the changes set out above are broken down below:

(a) The inclusion of the currency adjustment factor shall increase the present value of the defined benefit obligation by $40,243,099, resulting in positive past service cost.

(b) The payment of 12 per cent of the base salary for each service year after 1 January 2015 shall increase the present value of the defined benefit obligation by $18,044,064, resulting in positive past service cost. The valuation of the end-of-service benefit for local staff as of 31 December 2015 on the same assumptions (demographic and financial) used in prior year valuation resulted in an actuarial gain of $8.841 million (excluding the discount rate change during the year). This gain is largely driven by the fact that overall salaries increased at a lower rate than expected during the year 2015.

(Thousands of United States dollars)

	31 December 2015	31 December 2014
Opening balance as at 1 January	524 540	491 717
Interest costs for the year	28 233	23 163
Service costs for the year	40 711	34 810
Past service costs[a]	58 287	(8 949)
Discount rate change for the year[b]	29 011	–
Payments in the year	(21 906)	(13 932)
Actuarial (gains)/losses	(8 841)	(2 269)
Total	**650 035**	**524 540**

[a] Benefit enhancement due to the extension of age of retirement for area staff on an optional basis from 60 to 62 years, effective 1 January 2014. Past service costs for the year 2015 include the impact of the change in currency adjustment factor in the basic salary for staff in Gaza and the West Bank and the change in end-of-service payment percentage from 11 per cent to 12 per cent.

[b] Discount rate change from 4.75 per cent to 4.32 per cent is included in the actuarial gains (losses).

Key assumptions

15.15 The discount rate used was based on the currency and the term of the underlying liabilities. Where the benefit offered by the Agency provided protection for the fluctuation of the local currency against the United States dollar, the benefit was assumed to be in United States dollars and the applicable United States dollar discount rate was used. This has been the case for the Lebanon, West Bank and Jordan field offices and the Amman headquarters.

15.16 The discount rates and future escalation used, by field and currency, are as follows:

(Percentage)

Field	Currency	Currency protection	Discount rate	Future escalation
Gaza	United States dollar	No	4.32	2.50
Gaza headquarters	United States dollar	No	4.32	2.50
Jordan	Jordanian dinar	Yes (Jordanian dinar/United States dollar)	4.32	2.50
Amman headquarters	Jordanian dinar	Yes (Jordanian dinar/United States dollar)	4.32	2.50
West Bank	Jordanian dinar	Yes (Jordanian dinar/United States dollar)	4.32	2.50
Lebanon	Lebanese pound	Yes (Lebanese pound/United States dollar)	4.32	2.50
Syrian Arab Republic	United States dollar	No	4.32	2.50

15.17 The discount rates were set with reference to government bonds, high-quality corporate bonds and other instruments, depending on the currency, term and availability of such instruments for the currency under consideration. However, owing to the continuous low interest rate environment, the discount rate has been revised by management from 4.75 per cent to 4.32 per cent, which is consistent with the yields on investment grade corporate United States bonds with term to maturity, consistent with the duration of the end-of-service liability. The reduction in the discount rate has resulted in an actuarial loss of $29,016,266. Hence, the net actuarial loss for the year 2015 is $20,170,090, which represents 3.8 per cent of the opening balance of the provision.

Step increments

15.18 According to the current salary matrices of the Agency, step increments can be either an amount or a percentage. Subject to satisfactory performance, step increments are applied once a year for each employee until the employee reaches the maximum step level, which currently stands at 24.

Exchange rates as at 31 December 2015

15.19 The exchange rates used to convert local currencies to the United States dollar are based on the United Nations exchange rates, as follows: United States dollar, 1.000; Jordanian dinar, 0.708; Lebanese pound, 1,507.450; Syrian pound, 345.000.

Resignation rates

15.20 It is assumed that plan members will resign at the following rates per annum, according to attained age: less than 30 years, 3 per cent; for 30 to 34 years, 2 per cent; for 35 to 39 years, 1.5 per cent; and for 40 years and above, 0 per cent.

Early retirement rates

15.21 It is assumed that plan members will elect for early retirement according to the rates set out below.

(Percentage)

	Number of years since early retirement conditions have been satisfied			
Attained age	0	1	2	3 +
Less than 45	8.0	5.0	3.0	1.0
45-49	8.0	5.0	3.0	1.0
50-54	8.0	5.0	3.0	1.0
55-59	8.0	5.0	3.0	1.0

15.22 For the field of Jordan and the Amman headquarters, the assumed early retirement rates set out above were multiplied by 150 per cent.

Mortality

15.23 It is assumed that active members of the plan will experience in-service mortality in accordance with the 1996 United States Annuity 2000 mortality table for males and females.

Disability

15.24 It is assumed that disability cases will occur annually according to the probabilities set out below.

Disability rate

(Per thousand)

Age	Male	Female
Less than 45	0.50	0.75
45-54	1.00	1.50
55-62	1.50	2.25

International staff end-of-service liability

15.25 The separation costs of international staff funded from the regular budget of the United Nations (150 posts as at 31 December 2015 and 150 posts as at 31 December 2014) are borne by the regular budget, and no provision for these costs is made in the Agency's financial statements given that the liability will be borne by the United Nations. As a result, UNRWA has not disclosed after-service health insurance, repatriation grant or leave pay encashment in its financial statements. These liabilities relating to international staff should be included in the financial statements contained in the report of the Board of Auditors on the United Nations.

15.26 As a part of the implementation of IPSAS, UNRWA appointed an actuarial consultant to determine the employee liabilities for international staff members not funded from the United Nations regular budget. The value of liabilities for international staff not funded from the regular budget is summarized below.

(Thousands of United States dollars)

Benefit	31 December 2015	31 December 2014
Repatriation grant	827	809
Shipment	766	712
Travel	249	230
After-service health insurance	1 135	488
Outstanding annual leave	807	620
Total	**3 784**	**2 859**

Assumptions

15.27 The discount rate is assumed to be 4.32 per cent and future salary escalation is assumed to be 3 per cent. The general inflation considered for travel and shipment costs is 2 per cent. The after-service health insurance premium applied for United States nationality is assumed to increase by 6 per cent per annum and that applied for other nationalities is 4 per cent per annum. It is assumed that plan members will resign at the following rates per annum according to their attained ages: less than 30 years, 3 per cent; 30 to 34 years, 2 per cent; 35 to 39 years, 1.5 per cent; and 40 years and above, 0 per cent. It is assumed that rates of in-service mortality of active members of the plan will reflect those in the 1996 United States Annuity 2000 mortality table for males and females.

15.28 After-service health insurance coverage is optional for eligible former international project staff members and their dependants. The Agency's contribution to the after-service health insurance premium is set at 50 per cent with the rest paid by the former staff member. Aetna rates were used for international staff members not funded from the United Nations regular budget and holding United States citizenship, while Vanbreda rates were used for other nationalities. It is of note that only three employees are expected to qualify for this benefit on the assumption of no contract extension.

Note 16
Other current liabilities

Other current liabilities comprise the following:

(Thousands of United States dollars)

	31 December 2015	31 December 2014
Goods in transit payable	5 438	4 857
Donor refund payable	–	288
Total	**5 438**	**5 145**

Note 17
Advance contribution

The amount of contributions received in advance of the criteria for revenue recognition being met is as follows:

(Thousands of United States dollars)

	31 December 2015	31 December 2014
Received from Governments	45 957	1 119
Received from intergovernmental organizations	–	1 489
Received from United Nations organizations	213	–
Total	**46 170**	**2 608**

Note 18
Contingent liabilities, contingent assets and operating lease commitments

Contingent liabilities

18.1   The Agency's contingent liabilities as at 31 December 2015, compiled by the Legal Department, arise broadly from two categories: those in connection with personnel matters in respect of significant claims, litigation or arbitration, and those associated with contractual matters. Contractual matters relate mostly to claims pertaining to procurement or purchase orders and construction, and claims from proprietors of buildings rented by the Agency.

18.2   A number of personnel appeals which could involve the payment of salary and entitlements or other damages were pending with the UNRWA Dispute Tribunal and the United Nations Appeals Tribunal. The contingent liabilities relating to these appeals amounted to approximately $1.048 million as at 31 December 2015 (compared with $1.240 million as at 31 December 2014).

18.3   The contingent liabilities for commercial contracts amounted to approximately $179.428 million as at 31 December 2015 (compared with $153.297 million as at 31 December 2014).

Contingent assets

18.4   The Agency's contingent assets represent pledges for which donor agreements have been signed but with respect to which the criteria for revenue recognition have not been met. The total amount of contingent assets outstanding as at 31 December 2015 was $287.159 million (compared with $256.421 million as at 31 December 2014).

Operating lease commitments

18.5   Operating costs include lease payments in the amount of $3.779 million recognized as operating lease expenses during 2015 (compared with $3.403 million in 2014). The amount includes minimum lease payments. No contingent rent payments were made.

16-09975

18.6   The Agency holds principally cancellable operating leases. The operating lease agreements relate mainly to school premises, health centres, land and collective shelters for camps, field administrative offices, and warehouse and distribution centres. The total of future minimum lease payments is as follows:

(Thousands of United States dollars)

	31 December 2015	*31 December 2014*
Not later than one year	140	255
Later than one year and not later than five years	–	52
Later than five years	–	–
Total	**140**	**307**

18.7   Most of the operating lease agreements contain renewal clauses that enable the Agency to extend the terms of the leases at the end of the original terms. Some of the agreements have escalation clauses based on a fixed percentage increase or a fixed amount increase applied at prespecified intervals or dates in the future. No lease agreements contain purchase options.

18.8   The host Governments and some charitable organizations in the fields in which UNRWA operates provide the use of land for no or nominal rent to UNRWA for the benefit of Palestine refugees. The land is used to build schools, health centres or other UNRWA facilities that are administered by the Agency or in which it provides services.

18.9   These in-kind donations for the use of land have been valued at a fair value of $4.013 million in 2015 (compared with $3.981 million in 2014) and are included in non-exchange revenue and occupancy costs. The fair value for these in-kind donations was calculated using recently negotiated commercial leases that UNRWA holds for land. The average rental return on the capital value of land for commercial leases was applied to the capital value of land, as assessed by external surveyors, provided to UNRWA at no or nominal value.

18.10   The Agency received revenue of $3.031 million from sublease payments in 2015 (compared with $3.142 million in 2014). All subleases are cancellable and contain no contingent lease payments.

Note 19
Revolving loan fund

19.1   Restricted contributions received for on-lending purposes are transferred to the revolving loan fund for both the Microfinance Department and the microcredit community support programme. The revolving loan fund is included as a component of the Microfinance Department and microcredit community support programme reserve in the statement of changes in net assets/equity.

19.2   The composition of the revolving loan fund as at 31 December 2015 and 31 December 2014 was as follows:

(Thousands of United States dollars)

	31 December 2015	31 December 2014
Microfinance Department	24 325	24 324
Microcredit community support programme	3 428	3 238
Total	**27 753**	**27 562**

Note 20
Cash contributions revenue

Total cash contributions revenue by source received in 2015 and 2014 was as follows:

(Thousands of United States dollars)

	2015	2014
Governments	913 682	1 032 277
Intergovernmental organizations	181 848	176 220
Non-governmental organizations and other entities	19 562	40 750
United Nations organizations	44 531	43 278
Sundry	2 685	–
Total	**1 162 308**	**1 292 525**

Note 21
In-kind contributions revenue

Total in-kind contributions revenue by source received in 2015 and 2014 was as follows:

(Thousands of United States dollars)

	2015	2014
Governments	11 010	19 116
Intergovernmental organizations	–	13
Non-governmental organizations and other entities	3 992	8 468
United Nations organizations	1 419	1 066
Total	**16 421**	**28 663**

Note 22
Interest on loans

Interest on loans represents interest charged on loans issued by the Microfinance Department and the microcredit community support programme throughout the five fields. The composition of interest on loans in 2015 and 2014 was as follows:

(Thousands of United States dollars)

	2015	2014
Microfinance Department	9 421	7 783
Microcredit community support programme	280	266
Total	**9 701**	**8 049**

Note 23
Interest revenue

Interest revenue is recognized over the period during which it is earned. The amount of interest on bank deposits is $0.344 million in 2015 (compared with $0.453 million in 2014).

Note 24
Currency exchange gain/(loss)

Currency exchange gains or losses are realized and unrealized exchange gains or losses on the translation of non-United States dollar-denominated balances and transactions during the year.

(Thousands of United States dollars)

	2015	2014
Realized currency exchange rate gain	9 725	292
Unrealized currency exchange rate loss	(4 094)	(15 957)
Accounts receivable income realized exchange rate gain/(loss)	(918)	(678)
Total	**4 713**	**(16 343)**

Note 25
Programme support cost recovery

The Agency is entitled to a specific percentage of the expenditure incurred on certain projects in accordance with donor agreements. Programme support cost recoveries are recognized as income and represent the recovery of indirect costs incurred by the Agency in implementing the related projects. The total programme support cost recovery from projects revenue for 2015 is $50.867 million (compared with $49.226 million in 2014). The total revenue is offset by the cost of projects in 2015 by $50.706 million (compared with $49.128 million in 2014) and the remaining amount of programme support cost recovery is $0.161 million in 2015 (compared with $0.098 million in 2014) from Junior Professional Officer programmes).

Note 26
Miscellaneous revenue

26.1 Miscellaneous revenue comprised the following:

(Thousands of United States dollars)

	2015	2014 (restated)
Canteen lease revenue	3 031	3 142
Loss on income-producing activities	–	(13)
Sundries	4 827	8 334
Income received from United Nations agencies	98	168
Refunds to donors	(278)	(541)
Total	**7 678**	**11 090**

26.2 Refunds to donors represent amounts that have been recorded as revenue but are required to be refunded to donors in accordance with the terms of donor agreements.

Note 27
Wages, salaries and employee benefits

Wages, salaries and employee benefits consisted of the following:

(Thousands of United States dollars)

	2015	2014
International staff	45 145	43 739
Area staff		
Basic salaries, allowances and benefits	599 680	546 646
Area Staff Provident Fund contributions	55 533	52 403
Health-related expenses	9 583	8 712
Total	**709 941**	**651 500**

Note 28
Supplies and consumables

The composition of supplies and consumables in 2015 and 2014 was as follows:

(Thousands of United States dollars)

	2015	2014
Basic commodities	71 825	96 912
Clothing supplies	3 233	6 235
Fresh food	13 625	25 558
Medical supplies	23 551	23 302
Miscellaneous supplies	17 089	21 335
Replacement cost adjustments	2 639	–
Sport supplies	180	320
Textbooks and library books	1 435	5 433
Transportation supplies	9 016	6 932
Total	**142 593**	**186 027**

Note 29
Occupancy, utilities and premises costs

Occupancy, utilities and premises costs in 2015 and 2014 included the following:

(Thousands of United States dollars)

	2015	*2014*
Rental of premises	7 791	7 384
Maintenance of premises	9 464	7 562
Utilities	5 586	7 022
Total	**22 841**	**21 968**

Note 30
Contracted services

The composition of services expenses in 2015 and 2014 was as follows:

(Thousands of United States dollars)

	2015	*2014 (restated)*
Construction and equipment	49 353	64 450
Contractual costs	17 090	15 360
Hospital costs	28 399	19 732
Miscellaneous, including accruals	6 836	7 763
Consultancy costs	18 989	19 020
Demurrage and port charges	12 772	10 962
Training costs	5 269	3 691
Travel	1 495	2 582
Total	**140 203**	**143 560**

Note 31
Subsidies

31.1 Subsidies represent amounts paid to Palestine refugees for the following:

(Thousands of United States dollars)

	2015	*2014*
Cash subsidies to beneficiaries	187 877	174 869
Patient subsidies	5 793	5 187
Subsidies for the construction and repair of shelters	61 385	48 398
Subsidies payable to third party	6 109	7 257
Total	**261 164**	**235 711**

31.2 Cash subsidies paid to beneficiaries provide selective cash assistance for conflict-affected Palestine refugees in the Gaza Strip and the Syrian Arab Republic, food security and rent subsidies, whereas subsidies paid to third parties consist of cash disbursed by UNRWA to the community for activities that will improve the lives of the refugees.

Note 32
Provisions and write-offs

The composition of provisions and write-off expenses in 2015 and 2014 was as follows:

(Thousands of United States dollars)

	2015	2014
Provisions and write-off expenses on accounts receivable	18 364	17 524
Provision and write-off expenses on contributions receivable	4 275	817
Provisions and write-off expenses on loans receivable	704	1 117
Total	**23 343**	**19 458**

Note 33
Segment reporting

33.1　A segment is a distinguishable activity or group of activities for which it is appropriate to separately report financial information. Segment information is provided on several bases to reflect UNRWA objectives and activities. Full segment reporting is provided for sources of funds' segments. Segment expense reports are provided for (a) human development goals, (b) programmes and (c) geographical locations.

(a)　Sources of funds

33.2　A fund is an accounting entity established to account for transactions relating to a specified purpose or objective. Funds are segregated for the purpose of conducting specific activities or attaining certain objectives in accordance with special regulations, restrictions or limitations. The financial statements are prepared on a fund accounting basis, showing at the end of the period the aggregated position of all funds. Fund balances represent the accumulated residual amount of revenue and expenses.

33.3　The Agency's activities are financed through five fund groups. Each group of funds has differing parameters for utilization of the revenue.

33.4　The unearmarked fund is part of the UNRWA programme budget and is the principal means of financing the Agency's recurrent activities. The fund enables the Agency to meet obligations from authorized appropriations and is financed primarily by voluntary contributions and in-kind donations from Governments, intergovernmental and non-governmental bodies and host authorities.

33.5　The earmarked fund is also part of the UNRWA programme budget but its use is restricted to specific activities (e.g. direct support, cash and food assistance provided through the social safety net programme) that are undertaken during a defined time period within a defined budget.

33.6   The Microfinance Department fund is used to provide credit for enterprise activities, household consumption and housing needs that will improve the quality of life of householders and small-business owners and will help to sustain jobs, reduce poverty, empower women and provide income-generating opportunities for Palestine refugees.

33.7   Emergency appeal funds are used to address emergency needs through the delivery of emergency relief, for example, food aid, shelter and medical supplies. Funds are raised mainly through the consolidated appeals process and are to be utilized during specified time periods. Pursuant to implementation of the new enterprise resource planning system, emergency appeals funds for the Syrian Arab Republic were internally reclassified from the earmarked projects segment to the earmarked emergency appeals segment. This is also in line with donor reporting effective 2015.

33.8   Project funds are used to meet capital expenditure needs (e.g. school and health centre construction) or development needs to improve or supplement existing programmes and systems (e.g. environmental health improvement). Projects are undertaken to meet a specific objective, and contributions are time-bound and earmarked for specified purposes.

(b)   Human development goals

33.9   As part of its planning approach, UNRWA has four human development goals to provide it with direction in fulfilling its mission of helping Palestine refugees, with the aim of accomplishing the goals with efficient and effective governance. Fifteen strategic objectives that guide UNRWA core activities are grouped into the four human development goals, as follows:

- A long and healthy life, including the objectives of: (a) ensuring universal access to quality, comprehensive primary health care; (b) protecting and promoting family health; and (c) preventing and controlling diseases;

- Acquired knowledge and skills, including the objectives of: (a) ensuring universal access to and coverage of basic education; (b) enhancing education quality and outcomes against set standards; and (c) improving access to education opportunities for learners with special education needs;

- A decent standard of living, including the objectives of: (a) reducing abject poverty; (b) mitigating the effects of emergencies (both small-scale family and national crises) on individuals; (c) offering inclusive financial services and increased access to credit and savings facilities, especially for vulnerable groups such as women, youth and the poor; (d) improving employability; and (e) improving the urban environment through sustainable camp improvement and the upgrading of substandard infrastructure and accommodation;

- Human rights enjoyed to the fullest possible extent, including the objectives of: (a) ensuring that service delivery meets the protection needs of beneficiaries, including vulnerable groups; (b) safeguarding and advancing the rights of Palestine refugees by promoting respect for human rights, international humanitarian law and international refugee law; (c) strengthening the capacity of refugees to formulate and implement sustainable social services in their communities; and (d) ensuring that Palestine refugee registration and determination of eligibility for UNRWA services are carried out in accordance with relevant international standards;

- In addition to the above-mentioned goals, UNRWA aims for effective and efficient governance through providing overall direction and control and ensuring both efficient operations and effective financial and risk management.

(c) Programme

33.10 The Agency is functionally organized under four core programmes that provide direct services to UNRWA beneficiaries, led by executive direction and supported by support departments:

- The education programme provides basic and secondary education for learners with special education needs, and vocational and technical training. The programme has 10 vocational training centres, which provide skills training in such fields as pharmacy, plumbing, carpentry, business and computing. The programme offers in-service training and development for teachers to develop their professional qualifications and pre-service training for new teachers. The programme also encourages the progression of students to higher education by means of scholarships;

- The health programme provides a network of primary health-care facilities and mobile clinics that provide the foundation of its health services, offering preventive general medicine and specialist care services tailored for each stage of life. Although the programme is focused mainly on primary health care, it also helps Palestine refugees to gain access to secondary and tertiary health-care services. The environmental health subprogramme controls the quality of drinking water, provides sanitation and carries out vector and rodent control in refugee camps;

- The infrastructure and camp improvement programme addresses the deteriorating living conditions of Palestine refugees in camps. The programme promotes environmentally and socially sustainable neighbourhoods. UNRWA repairs shelters and, in coordination with the host Governments, plans for rehousing and reconstruction projects after demolitions caused by armed conflict or other emergencies. The programme manages the construction and maintenance of all UNRWA facilities and installations.

- The relief and social services programme provides a range of direct and indirect social protection services for Palestine refugees. The relief services subprogramme provides social safety-net assistance that includes basic food support, cash subsidies and additional family income supplements for the most vulnerable Palestine refugees caught in the cycle of abject poverty. It also provides selective cash assistance, such as one-off cash grants for basic household needs in family emergencies. In addition, the subprogramme provides direct aid during emergencies caused by violence and political unrest, along with shelter rehabilitation in coordination with other programmes. The social services subprogramme promotes community-based action that enables particularly vulnerable refugees to become more self-reliant. The programme particularly addresses the needs of women, refugees with disabilities, young people and the elderly. It also helps vulnerable refugees through its microcredit programme, which is managed by community-based organizations;

- Executive direction manages all aspects of the Agency's work to ensure efficient implementation of UNRWA mandates to provide services and humanitarian assistance to Palestine refugees, and to non-refugees on an exceptional basis, and to maintain the commitment of the international community to the social and economic well-being of Palestine refugees. Executive direction responsibilities include the effective management of oversight, legal support, fundraising, advocacy and outreach to external interlocutors;

- The support departments assist the Commissioner-General in the smooth running of the Agency and ensure effective management of personnel and financial resources, administrative services and internal communication.

(d) Geographical locations

33.11 Although UNRWA goals and services are delivered primarily within a programme approach, the Agency's operations are managed on a field basis. UNRWA operates in five fields: Jordan, Lebanon, the Syrian Arab Republic, the Gaza Strip and the West Bank. Each field provides similar services but is distinctive to some extent, owing to the particular political humanitarian and economic contexts in which it operates and the status and rights enjoyed by the Palestine refugees in it.

33.12 The operations of the five field offices which, together with UNRWA headquarters, provide services directly to Palestine refugees are described below:

- *Gaza field office.* The Gaza Strip has a population of more than 1.8 million, including some 1,311,920 registered Palestine refugees. The field office supports eight camps, 257 schools, two vocational and technical training centres, 22 primary health centres, seven community rehabilitation centres and seven women's programme centres. The ongoing blockade of the Gaza Strip has severely affected the economy and the enjoyment by Palestine refugees of a range of human rights;

- *Lebanon field office.* Some 458,360 Palestine refugees are registered with UNRWA in Lebanon, with many living in refugee camps. The field office supports 12 camps, 67 schools, two vocational and technical training centres, 27 primary health centres, one rehabilitation centre and eight women's programme centres. Palestine refugees in Lebanon do not enjoy several basic human rights; for example, they have restricted access to the local labour market;

- *Syrian Arab Republic field office.* UNRWA is mandated to provide services to more than 534,650 Palestine refugees living in the official camps and the three unofficial camps in the Syrian Arab Republic. The ongoing armed conflict in the Syrian Arab Republic has affected the economy, which in turn has had an impact on the Palestine refugee community. The field office supports nine camps, 100 schools, the Damascus Training Centre, 26 primary health centres, five community rehabilitation centres and 12 women's programme centres. While Palestine refugees have many of the rights of Syrian citizens, including access to social services provided by the Government, development indicators reveal that they lag behind the host population in key areas; Palestine refugees have also been vulnerable to the ongoing conflict. Many have been displaced within the Syrian Arab Republic, while thousands of others have fled to neighbouring countries, including Lebanon and Jordan. The situation remains volatile, with numbers and needs constantly changing, but despite the many challenges, UNRWA is continuing its emergency relief, health and education services in the Syrian Arab Republic. In Lebanon and Jordan, the Agency is also trying to provide for the needs of those fleeing the conflict;

- *Jordan field office*. Over 2,144,230 Palestine refugees are registered in Jordan. The field office supports 10 camps, 172 schools, two vocational and technical training centres, 25 primary health centres, eight community rehabilitation centres and 12 women's programme centres. All Palestine refugees in Jordan have full citizenship, with the exception of some 140,000 Palestine refugees originally from Gaza, who are eligible for temporary passports but are not entitled to vote or to work in government;

- *West Bank field office*. The West Bank covers an area of 5,500 square km and has an estimated population of 2.4 million, around 792,080 of whom are registered Palestine refugees. One quarter of the registered Palestine refugees live in 19 refugee camps, with most others living in West Bank towns and villages. The field office supports 19 camps, 96 schools, two vocational and technical training centres, 43 primary health centres, 15 community rehabilitation centres and 18 women's programme centres. West Bank refugees have been hard hit by closures imposed on the West Bank by the Israeli authorities; historically, they have been largely dependent on income from work inside Israel;

- *UNRWA headquarters* covers three locations: the Gaza Strip, East Jerusalem and Amman. The headquarters organization includes the Department of Planning, the Department of Administrative Support, the Department of Internal Oversight Services, the Department of Human Resources, the Department of Legal Affairs, the Executive Office, the Finance Department, the Enterprise Resource Planning Department and the External Relations and Communications Department, as well as the departments of education, health, relief and social services, infrastructure and camp improvement, and microfinance. The headquarters function is also carried out at representative offices in New York, Washington, D.C., and Brussels, and at a liaison office in Cairo.

(e) Basis of pricing for inter-segment transfers and charges

33.13 Programme support costs are incurred by UNRWA in support of the implementation of its non-regular budget activities that cannot be directly attributed to specific activities, projects or programmes. Programme support costs represent administrative, managerial, logistical and other support costs, including costs relating to staff recruitment, budgetary and financial control, information and communications technology support, and actions in respect of procurement transport and warehousing.

33.14 Programme support costs represent a recovery of project expenditures to ensure that non-regular activities do not constitute financial costs in terms of the Agency's regular budget.

33.15 Programme support costs at a uniform standard rate of 11 per cent are usually charged against all contributions for non-regular budget activities except for those of the Microfinance Department, with respect to which a standard rate of 6 per cent is charged on the Department's running costs, excluding staff costs.

Segment reporting by fund: financial position as at 31 December 2015

(Thousands of United States dollars)

	Unearmarked activities	Earmarked activities					
	Programme budget	Restricted funds	Microfinance Department	Emergency appeals	Projects	Inter-fund balances	Total
Assets							
Current assets							
Cash and cash equivalents	41 758	1 553	8 976	168 670	87 827	–	308 784
Short-term loans receivable	–	–	21 351	–	1 334	–	22 685
Contributions receivable	2 574	–	–	7 437	29 628	–	39 639
Accounts receivable	33 473	–	46	110	6 248	(6 108)	33 769
Other current assets	3 293	14	380	108	263	–	4 058
Operational Microfinance Department account with UNRWA	–	673	–	–	–	(673)	–
Inventories	16 984	4 497	–	56 227	24 200	–	101 908
Derivative financial instruments	7 658	–	–	–	–	–	7 658
Non-current assets							
Other non-current assets	188	–	–	–	–	–	188
Long-term loans receivable	–	–	2 471	–	937	–	3 408
Property, plant and equipment	423 747	1 699	237	817	38 278	–	464 778
Intangible assets	35 654	254	394	224	–	–	36 526
Total assets	**565 328**	**8 690**	**33 855**	**233 593**	**188 715**	**(6 781)**	**1 023 401**
Liabilities							
Current liabilities							
Payables and accruals	30 628	905	442	21 907	13 439	(28)	67 293
Employee benefits	76 896	–	454	–	–	–	77 350
Derivative financial liability	1 085	–	–	–	–	–	1 085
Operational Microfinance Department account with UNRWA	–	–	673	–	–	(673)	–
Other current liabilities	1 525	1	–	3 912	–	–	5 438
Advance contributions	52 278	–	–	–	–	(6 108)	46 170
Non-current liabilities							
Employee benefits	616 570	–	3 517	–	–	–	620 087
Other non-current liabilities	–	–	9 875	–	–	–	9 875
Total liabilities	**778 982**	**906**	**14 961**	**25 819**	**13 439**	**(6 809)**	**827 298**
Net assets	**(213 653)**	**7 784**	**18 895**	**207 773**	**175 276**	**28**	**196 103**

	Unearmarked activities	Earmarked activities					
	Programme budget	Restricted funds	Microfinance Department	Emergency appeals	Projects	Inter-fund balances	Total
Revaluation and other reserves	(23 498)	–	–	–	–	476	(23 022)
Capital reserve: microcredit community support programme and Microfinance Department	–	–	24 324	–	3 429	–	27 753
Accumulated surplus/deficit	(190 156)	7 784	(5 428)	207 773	171 847	(448)	191 372
Total net assets/equity	**(213 653)**	**7 784**	**18 896**	**207 773**	**175 276**	**28**	**196 103**

Segment reporting by fund: financial performance as at 31 December 2015

(Thousands of United States dollars)

	Unearmarked activities	Earmarked activities					
	Programme budget	Restricted funds	Microfinance Department	Emergency appeals	Projects	Inter-fund balances	Total
Revenue							
Cash contributions	566 369	2 734	–	413 077	180 128	–	1 162 308
In-kind contributions	–	8 489	–	5 313	2 619	–	16 421
Interest on loans	1	–	9 420	–	280	–	9 701
Interest on bank deposits	267	–	77	–	–	–	344
Other revenue							
Foreign currency exchange gain	8 182	(1)	(677)	(323)	(2 468)	–	4 713
Programme support cost recovery	50 867	–	–	–	–	(50 706)	161
Financial derivative gain	11 404	–	–	–	–	–	11 404
Miscellaneous revenue	1 963	4 877	748	240	(256)	106	7 678
Total revenue	**639 053**	**16 099**	**9 568**	**418 307**	**180 303**	**(50 600)**	**1 212 730**
Expenses							
Wages, salaries and employee benefits	605 051	1 255	6 362	58 095	38 972	206	709 941
Supplies and consumables	46 522	8 779	135	78 777	8 377	3	142 593
Occupancy, utilities and premises costs	8 732	7 751	392	4 189	1 776	1	22 841
Contracted services	42 916	1 304	1 278	35 460	59 286	(40)	140 203
Programme support costs	110	230	–	39 826	10 540	(50 706)	–
Subsidies	11 665	(839)	–	202 482	47 856	–	261 164
Depreciation	29 960	–	364	–	–	–	30 324
Provisions and write-offs	18 364	–	692	–	4 277	10	23 343
Loss on disposal	3 261	–	–	–	–	–	3 261
Impairment of property, plant and equipment	104	–	–	–	–	–	104
Total expenses	**766 685**	**18 480**	**9 222**	**418 830**	**171 084**	**(50 527)**	**1 333 775**
Surplus/(deficit) for the year	**(127 631)**	**(2 381)**	**346**	**(523)**	**9 218**	**(74)**	**(121 045)**

Segment reporting by human development goal: expenses as at 31 December 2015

(Thousands of United States dollars)

	Long and healthy life	Acquired knowledge and skills	Decent standard of living	Human rights enjoyed to the fullest	Effective and efficient governance and support in the Agency	Unallocated human development goal	Inter-fund balances	Total
Wages, salaries and employee benefits	106 626	399 975	62 502	9 327	131 305	–	206	709 941
Supplies and consumables	22 302	9 435	94 218	3 563	13 072	–	3	142 593
Occupancy, utilities and premises costs	1 761	9 417	4 556	514	6 592	–	1	22 841
Contracted services	36 190	14 002	52 275	2 680	32 756	2 340	(40)	140 203
Programme support costs	3 513	5 934	34 198	1 391	5 590	80	(50 706)	–
Subsidies	6 063	5 940	246 887	2 018	255	–	–	261 164
Depreciation	3 387	13 683	2 752	644	9 857	1	–	30 324
Provisions and write-offs	–	–	694	–	22 639	–	10	23 343
Loss on disposal	7	3 241	–	10	3	–	–	3 261
Impairment of property, plant and equipment	40	55	9	–	–	–	–	104
Total	**179 889**	**461 682**	**498 091**	**20 147**	**222 071**	**2 422**	**(50 527)**	**1 333 775**

Segment reporting by programme: expenses as at 31 December 2015

(Thousands of United States dollars)

	Education	Health	Infrastructure and camp improvement	Relief and social services	Support department	Executive direction	Inter-fund balances	Total
Wages, salaries and employee benefits	445 838	77 833	30 663	27 848	68 546	59 007	206	709 941
Supplies and consumables	11 896	24 603	1 032	93 457	8 342	3 260	3	142 593
Occupancy, utilities and premises costs	11 149	1 573	1 791	2 636	4 937	754	1	22 841
Contracted services	15 292	33 103	29 393	29 287	20 607	12 561	(40)	140 203
Programme support costs	6 076	3 389	2 166	32 028	2 300	4 747	(50 706)	–
Subsidies	3 775	6 201	3 319	227 928	(817)	20 758	–	261 164
Depreciation	15 501	2 613	1 225	1 483	8 764	739	–	30 324
Provisions and write-offs	–	–	–	694	22 639	–	10	23 343
Loss on disposal	3 241	2	5	10	3	–	–	3 261
Impairment of property, plant and equipment	55	40	–	9	–	–	–	104
Total	**512 822**	**149 357**	**69 594**	**415 380**	**135 323**	**101 826**	**(50 527)**	**1 333 775**

Segment reporting by geographical location: expenses as at 31 December 2015

(Thousands of United States dollars)

Expenses	Gaza field	Lebanon field	Syrian Arab Republic field	Jordan field	West Bank field	Headquarters	Inter-fund balances	Total
Wages, salaries and employee benefits	290 337	79 427	55 982	127 092	120 521	36 376	206	709 941
Supplies and consumables	81 266	9 984	25 994	13 313	11 525	508	3	142 593
Occupancy, utilities and premises costs	6 133	2 933	1 400	6 492	5 129	753	1	22 841
Contracted services	45 318	57 281	7 233	4 723	10 337	15 351	(40)	140 203
Programme support costs	27 500	4 298	13 080	1 639	3 896	293	(50 706)	–
Subsidies	115 354	35 491	79 929	11 934	17 608	848	–	261 164
Depreciation	12 831	2 957	1 892	2 549	4 673	5 423	–	30 324
Provisions and write-offs	10 955	2	26	451	1 872	10 028	10	23 343
Loss on disposal	3 259	–	2	–	–	–	–	3 261
Impairment of property, plant and equipment	–	–	104	–	–	–	–	104
Total	**592 953**	**192 372**	**185 642**	**168 192**	**175 562**	**69 581**	**(50 527)**	**1 333 775**

Note 34
Presentation of budget information

34.1   The budget figures for UNRWA are determined on a modified cash basis and disclosed in the statement of comparison of budget and actual amounts (statement V) as the original budget derived from the 2014-2015 programme budget (Blue Book). The UNRWA budget includes the core requirements funded through the programme budget (previously called General Fund), as endorsed by the General Assembly, which, if exceeded, requires submission to the General Assembly; in-kind donations; and the projects budget, where allocation varies based on donor response.

34.2   As compared with the Blue Book budget, the programme budget, made available at the beginning of each financial period, reflects reduced requirements based on the end-of-year income forecast and acceptable cash shortfall. However, for the projects budget, resources are made available when contributions are received and/or, on an exceptional basis, when pledges are confirmed by donors, by means of a signed agreement, for approved project proposals.

34.3   With the adoption of IPSAS, UNRWA internally adopted an accrual budgeting system based on IPSAS. However, in compliance with the Financial Rules and Regulations, the final budget set out in financial statement V still refers to a modified cash basis budget and is used for comparison with the actual amounts.

34.4   The UNRWA budget encompasses three main entities (funding portal types): the programme budget, funded mainly by voluntary contributions, along with 150 international staff funded through the United Nations regular budget from assessed contributions; an in-kind donations budget; and the projects budget.

34.5   The Agency's budget structure follows a results-based budgeting format, as reflected in the annual operational plans which are derived from the medium-term strategy for the period 2010-2015.

34.6   The budgets and accounts of UNRWA are arranged on different accounting bases. The statement of financial position, the statement of financial performance, the statement of changes in net assets and the statement of cash flow are prepared on a full accrual basis, using a classification based on the nature of expenses in the statement of financial performance, whereas the statement of comparison of budget and actual amounts (statement V) is prepared on a modified cash basis of accounting.

34.7   As required under IPSAS 24, the actual amounts presented on a comparable basis to the budget shall, where the financial statements and the budget are not prepared on a comparable basis, be reconciled to the actual amounts presented in the financial statements, identifying separately any basis, timing and entity differences. There may also be differences in formats and classification schemes adopted for the presentation of the financial statements and the budget.

34.8   Basis differences occur when the approved budget is prepared on a basis other than the accounting basis, as stated in paragraph 34.6 above.

34.9   Timing differences occur when the budget period differs from the reporting period reflected in the financial statements. There are no timing differences for UNRWA for purposes of comparison of budget and actual amounts.

34.10   Entity differences occur when the budget omits funds that are part of the entity for which the financial statements are prepared.

34.11   Presentation differences are due to differences in the format and classification schemes adopted for presentation of the statement of cash flow and the statement of comparison of budget and actual amounts.

34.12   Reconciliation between the actual amounts on a comparable basis in the statement of comparison of budget and actual amounts (statement V) and the actual amounts in the statement of cash flow (statement IV) for the period ended 31 December 2015 is presented below.

(Thousands of United States dollars)

	Operating	Investing	Financing	Total
Actual amounts on a comparable basis (statement V)	746 487	153 125	–	899 612
Basis differences	112 874	(206 145)	(283)	(93 554)
Timing differences	–	–	–	–
Entity differences	33 082	(829)	474	32 727
Presentation differences	(835 455)	–	–	(835 455)
Actual amounts in the statement of cash flow (statement IV)	**56 988**	**(53 849)**	**191**	**3 330**

34.13   Open commitments, including open purchase orders and net cash flows from operating, investing and financing activities, are presented as basis differences.

Revenue that does not form part of the statement of comparison of budget and actual amounts is reflected as presentation differences. Entity differences occur as the approved budget, as noted above, includes the programme budget, the in-kind donations budget and the projects budget. The cash flow statement also includes the emergency appeals fund, the Microfinance Department fund and the earmarked fund of the programme budget.

34.14 Budget amounts have been presented on a classification based on the nature of expenses in accordance with the approved 2014-2015 programme budget, as recommended by the Advisory Committee on Administrative and Budgetary Questions and endorsed by the General Assembly.

(Thousands of United States dollars)

	Total expenses
Actual amounts on a comparable basis (statement V)	899 612
Basis differences	56 648
Timing differences	–
Entity differences	377 515
Actual amounts in the statement of financial performance (statement II)	**1 333 775**

Explanations of material differences

34.15 Explanations of material differences between the original budget and the final budget, and between the final budget and the actual amounts, are presented below.

Original and final budgets (income and expense/capital expenditure)

34.16 The original budget of expenditure is the budget as published in the Blue Book, while the final budget of expenditure is the approved 2015 budget allocation at year-end.

34.17 The 2015 programme budget, as reflected in the Blue Book for 2014-2015, amounted to $982.2 million (modified cash basis). This is disclosed in financial statement V as "original" budget. On a modified cash basis, the final 2015 programme budget was $1,083.3 million, representing an increase of $101.1 million, or 10.3 per cent. This is disclosed in financial statement V as "final" budget. The $101.1 million is a reflection of the increase in the final budget owing to an increase in the final projects budget from $238.4 million to $379.5 million, including restricted funds (earmarked projects).

Utilization of the budget

34.18 The variation in the budgetary utilization of the different budget cost components is due to various factors, such as management actions to reduce the cash shortfall, the depreciation of the Israeli sheqel, compared with the budgeted exchange rate, improved alignment of cost recovery, cash distribution from the social safety net programme and other budget reserves. The utilization rate against the key various cost components rates is as follows:

- *Staff costs*. Implementation rate is 89.1 per cent. The underutilization of $50.2 million is due to: (a) lower vacancy rate for international staff (funded by assessed contributions) and no commitment of staff costs in the new enterprise resource planning system; (b) underspending under fixed-term area staff, daily paid and limited duration contracts by $30.4 million, owing to management actions adopted to bridge the cash shortfall; (c) the depreciation of the Israeli sheqel compared with the budgeted exchange rate by +$7.9 million, with part of the savings offset by a loss on Israeli sheqel/United States dollar hedges; and (d) the severance cash pay-out was underspent by +$7.7 million due to the increase in the number of early voluntary separations, under the policy introduced during 2015;

- *Supplies*. Implementation rate is 83.0 per cent. The underutilization of $15.0 million is due to timing variance and the late receipt of related project funds at the year-end, resulting in the phasing over of the projects budget to 2016;

- *Maintenance of premises and equipment*. Implementation rate is 78.4 per cent. The underspending of $46.1 million is due to the late receipt of several donor project pledges and other donor project pledges towards Gaza reconstruction, in addition to the time lag in access of goods and services to the Occupied Palestinian Territory in Gaza. The outstanding available budget at 2015 year-end was carried forward to 2016;

- *Training, travel, administrative services and consultancy*. Implementation rate is 74.5 per cent. The underutilization is due to continuous management actions adopted to meet the cash shortfall;

- *Hospital and miscellaneous services*. Implementation rate is 86.2 per cent. The underspending is due to projects related to service purchase orders yet to be implemented in the next financial period, in line with the projects' lifespan, and extended hospital contracts, in particular in Lebanon field office;

- *Subsidies to hardship cases, subsidies to patients and third parties*. The implementation rate is 86.1 per cent. The underspending of cash subsidies is due to timing variance dependent on the actual cash receipt of funds from donor-funded projects;

- *Reserves*. The reserves reflect the impact of management actions and improved alignment of cost recovery with emergency appeal projects, chiefly under the emergency appeal for the Syrian Arab Republic.

Note 35
Going concern

35.1 The accompanying financial statements have been prepared on the assumption that the Agency will continue to operate as a going concern. As shown in the financial statements, however, the Agency experienced a net deficit of $121.045 million in 2015 compared to a net gain of $43.692 million in 2014. The factors set out below provide evidence as to the continuing nature of the Agency as a going concern.

35.2 The Agency has total net assets of $196.103 million in 2015 (compared with $328.667 million in 2014) and total current assets exceed total current liabilities by $321.165 million in 2015 (compared with $349.365 million in 2014). The balance of cash and cash equivalents held by the Agency as at 31 December 2015 was $308.784 million (compared with $305.454 million in 2014). In addition, as described in note 18, the Agency, as at 31 December 2015, had contingent assets in the amount of $287.159 million (compared with $256.421 million as at 31 December 2014), relating to contributions from donors for which the agreements had been signed but the criteria for revenue recognition had not yet been met.

35.3 With the exception of 150 international staff posts funded by the General Assembly through the regular budget of the United Nations, the Agency's operations are funded by voluntary contributions from Member States and other donors for the support of its ongoing programmes and activities. All key donors reaffirm their support every six months at a semi-annual meeting of the Advisory Commission. UNRWA is also widening its donor base, strengthening relationships with Arab donors and engaging new private partners and countries to build presence in emerging markets, while further deepening relations with traditional donors.

35.4 Given the history of the Agency and the continuous efforts of management to mobilize resources for its operations, there is no substantial threat to the Agency's overall ability to operate as a going concern for the foreseeable future.

35.5 In 2013, as part of a strategic, medium-term approach, UNRWA began to develop its next medium-term strategy and 2016 will be the start of a new six-year strategic planning framework. The medium-term strategy 2016-2021 has similarities to the medium-term strategy 2010-2015, but also contains some very important improvements, including improvements to reflect the strategic development goals.

35.6 Funding the operations of the unearmarked activities of the programme budget has presented the greatest challenge to the Agency in recent years. As reflected in the segment reporting by fund, unearmarked activities incurred a deficit of $127.631 million as at 31 December 2015 (compared with a deficit of $30.383 million as at 31 December 2014). The net assets of the programme budget reflected a net deficit of $213.653 million as at 31 December 2015 (compared with a net deficit of $95.009 million as at 31 December 2014). The Agency is actively seeking contributions to support its unearmarked activities in order to sustain core operations.

Note 36
Related parties

36.   Related parties for UNRWA include:

(a)   The Area Staff Provident Fund, as it is controlled by the Agency;

(b)   The United Nations Secretariat, given that it exercises significant influence over UNRWA because, inter alia, the salaries, related expenditures and liabilities of the majority of the Agency's international staff, including its key management personnel, are paid from the regular budget of the United Nations;

(c)   Key management personnel, who include the members of the Management Committee, have authority with respect to planning, directing and controlling the activities of the Agency (or significant parts thereof). The major classes of key management personnel are Commissioner-General/Deputy Commissioner-General and field/headquarters directors. The aggregate remuneration paid to key management personnel includes net salaries, post adjustment, entitlements such as allowances, grants and subsidies, and employer pension and health insurance contributions. Key management personnel remuneration incorporates housing allowances and representation allowances paid as part of salaries, despite the presence of a representative aspect to these allowances. Transactions conducted with key management personnel in 2015 are summarized as follows:

(Thousands of United States dollars)

Number of individuals	Total remuneration	Outstanding advances against entitlements	Outstanding loans	Number of individuals
Key management personnel	25	4 960	135	–

(d) No close family members of key management personnel were employed by the Agency during the year;

(e) Advances are those made against entitlements in accordance with UNRWA area and international staff rules and regulations. Advances against entitlements are widely available to all UNRWA staff.

Note 37
Subsequent events

Limited demonstrations and protests in the Syrian Arab Republic in early 2011, arising from the so-called Arab Spring, developed into full-scale armed conflict by June 2012. The incessant conflict in the Syrian Arab Republic has continued into 2014 and 2015, affecting the economy and the stability of the region. The decrease in the value of the Syrian pound and the increase in the costs of basic commodities, along with ongoing conflict and physical damage to Agency assets, continue to affect UNRWA operations in the region. There is no indication of a final resolution. Consequently it is not possible to assess the future development of the value of the Syrian pound.

Note 38
Date and approval

The financial statements and notes were certified as correct and approved by the Director of Finance and were issued on 31 March 2016.

16-09975 (E)   170816

Please recycle